Trout Flies for
the 21st Century

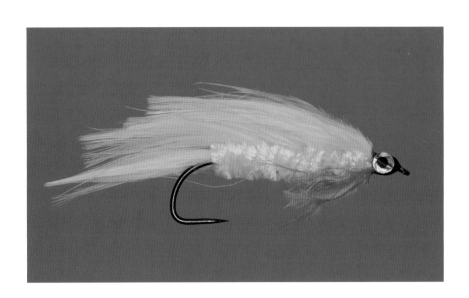

Fly Tyer

Trout Flies for the 21st Century

Over 200 Essential Patterns That Catch Fish Anywhere, Anytime

Dick Talleur

To Lee Mason —
Stiff hackles and tight lines always.
D. Talleur

THE LYONS PRESS
Guilford, Connecticut
An imprint of The Globe Pequot Press

Fly Tyer, the world's leading fly-tying magazine, is proud to bring you *Fly Tyer* Books published by The Lyons Press.

The Lyons Press is an imprint of The Globe Pequot Press.

Interior photos by Dick Talleur
Text designed by Peter Holm, Sterling Hill Productions

Library of Congress Cataloging-in-Publication Data

Talleur, Richard W.
 Trout flies for the 21st century : over 200 essential patterns that
catch fish anywhere, anytime / Dick Talleur.
    p. cm.
 Includes bibliographical references.
 ISBN 978-1-59921-259-3
 1. Fly tying. 2. Flies, Artificial. 3. Trout fishing. I. Title.
 SH451.T2918 2008
 688.7'9124—dc22

                        2007051742

Printed in China

10 9 8 7 6 5 4 3 2 1

To Vera A. Talleur and her son, Yuri Y. Kovalenko,
for leaving their Russian homeland and
coming to America to be my family.

With love, Dick

CONTENTS

FOREWORD

I was excited when the folks at The Lyons Press approached me with the concept to collaborate with *Fly Tyer* magazine on a new series of books. Lyons Press has a long and storied history of creating truly wonderful fly-fishing books; many have become classics that will be read by generations of fly anglers and tiers. *Fly Tyer* is home to the best authors and photographers specializing in the craft of fly tying, and I knew this was a golden opportunity to further showcase their talents.

The first task was to select the authors who would participate in this important project. It's no surprise that Dick Talleur topped the list. Dick has been a fly fisherman for half a century and has been tying flies for almost as long. While at heart he's a trout angler, Dick has created and tested many original patterns for catching salmon, bass, panfish, and most varieties of saltwater game fish. Dick has fished widely, from his home waters in New York's Catskill and Adirondack Mountains to England, Iceland, Ireland, New Zealand, Chile, Russia, the Bahamas, and beyond. Once upon a time, Dick even managed a major fly-tying factory in Thailand, where he learned the secret art of production tying. Today, when he's in the mood, Dick can crank out half-a-dozen flies in the time it takes me to make one.

Dick has probably contributed more articles to *Fly Tyer* than any other author; he was one of the first to appear in the magazine in the 1970s, and he remains one of our most cherished writers. In fact, it's just possible that Dick has contributed more books and articles to the fly-fishing literature than anyone in the history of the sport. Dick is always eager to share his hard-earned knowledge, and he gives presentations at fly-fishing shows, appears at clubs, and teaches fly-tying classes.

Trout Flies for the 21st Century is the first volume in the new *Fly Tyer* Library of fly-fishing books. In this book, Dick argues that fishing pressure, stocking, and new methods of angling have forever changed our sport, and that we need new patterns to meet this challenge. *Trout Flies for the 21st Century* is chockfull of original and updated classic patterns featuring the latest tying materials and methods. Tie these flies, and you will catch more fish.

Trout Flies for the 21st Century is an important book for another reason. This year, 2008, is *Fly Tyer* magazine's thirtieth anniversary. I can't imagine a more fitting tribute than to have a longtime friend of our magazine write a book about the future of fly tying. It is indeed a wonderful coincidence that this also is the first volume in the *Fly Tyer* Library.

Dick Talleur is a splendid ambassador for the sport of fly fishing and the craft of fly tying. His friendship has enriched my life in many ways, and I know that *Trout Flies for the 21st Century* will enrich yours.

Good tying and fishing, and I'll see you on the water.

David Klausmeyer
Editor
Fly Tyer magazine

PREFACE

So much has changed since I started waving the long rod over trout waters fifty years ago. The so-called tailrace fisheries, whereby cold water is bottom-released from dams, has turned catfish rivers into premium trout streams. For example, the White River in Arkansas produced the world-record brown trout not many years ago.

Catch-and-release, aka "no-kill," areas have had a profound effect on the quality of today's trout fishing. Trout that would have formerly been deposited in a creel now live to grow large, reproduce, and possibly die of old age. I know of a river within a three-hour drive of downtown Manhattan that harbored a nineteen-pound brown trout; the fish was captured and weighed during an electroshocking census. Even where regulations permit fish to be taken, many anglers release all of them anyway. This means that we not only have bigger trout to fish for, we have smarter ones as well.

Better management of hatcheries has also made a contribution. Improved foods produce healthier, stronger, prettier trout. Some private hatcheries grow trout that are almost indistinguishable from wild ones. Sure, we all love wild-trout fisheries, but they are quite limited. Hatchery-raised fish support the bulk of today's trout resources, and we should be very thankful for them.

With this book, I hope to bring you a wide selection of flies that are productive in today's trout-fishing environment. This doesn't mean that all of these flies are new and/or unique, although some of them certainly are. There are many fly patterns that have been around for quite a while that still work great. Many of these will be included, along with tips on tying techniques and new materials that make tying these flies easier and produce better results.

While this is essentially a pattern book, supplemental information—and in some instances, step-by-step photographs—will be provided for purposes of clarity. Some flies, especially the more innovative ones, have a key step or procedure that is critical and would be difficult for the tier to figure out without a bit of show-and-tell. In some cases, I've tied the flies larger than I would for fishing. This is a concession to photography, as I want to be able to show as much detail as possible.

In order to cover a wide variety of useful flies, I've solicited a lot of input from shop owners and guides around the country, as well as fishing friends in various areas. Thus, while I haven't fished all of the patterns in the book, I have assurances that the flies are highly productive. And many of them, while they are associated with a particular watershed, are effective most anywhere. For example, Marla Blair's simple yet deadly Jailbird, which performs so well on the hard-fished Farmington River, also takes fish in diverse environments. It's proven its effectiveness on rivers throughout the Rocky Mountains and even works on Great Lakes steelhead in New York's infamous Salmon River.

I love beautiful flies and masterful fly tying as much as anyone, but the emphasis here is not on cosmetics. I've tied the majority of the flies myself, and they are dressed the same as the ones I fish with. As for those flies that were sent to me by others, I've tried to photograph them as the tiers have tied them, as this is what those people fish with.

I have tried to identify the originators of all of the fly patterns, living or passed on. I have a particular gripe with appropriation of the work of others. It's impossible to patent fly patterns, and even to copyright the name at the current rate of $45 per application affords little protection. So we tiers should do our best to give credit where it's due.

Having said that, we must recognize that with many thousands of talented and creative people tying flies these days, it's not uncommon for two or more tiers to come up with the same or similar answers to the same problems. If anything in this book that I represent as being my own innovation actually appears to be duplication of something another tier came up with, I apologize, with assurances that it was not intentional.

A word about some of the items specified in the dressings: You'll see that I use a lot of Uni products, Daiichi hooks, and Whiting Farms feathers. That's because I've worked with these companies for a very long time, and these are the materials I have in my personal inventory. They are very good, but they are also not the only materials out there, so please feel free to use whatever works for you.

Credo: If it eats grass, gives milk, and goes "moo," it's a cow.

Materials that look and behave alike are functionally the same.

ACKNOWLEDGMENTS

I wish to express my most sincere thanks to the following people, in no particular order:

Dr. Tom Whiting of Whiting Farms, Delta, Colorado, for hackle feathers beyond anything we could ever have hoped for in past years. Angler's Sport Group of Elba, New York, for the wonderful Daiichi hooks and the generous support over many years. Uni Products of Ste. Melanie, Quebec, Canada, for their superb threads and similar products, and also for their kind support. John Albright of the HMH Vise Company for providing me with an outstanding instrument with which to tie my flies.

Jeff Curtis of Curtis Wright Outfitters, Weaverville, North Carolina, for four patterns that perform well in the wild-trout and delayed-harvest fisheries of the Great Smokies. Jack Gartside, fly designer and tier extraordinaire, for advice and counsel on how to properly dress his original patterns, six of which appear in this book.

Dave Goulet, longtime proprietor of the Classic and Custom Fly Shop on Connecticut's Farmington River, for six unique patterns represented in this book by flies that Dave tied himself. Buddy Knight, noted guide/tier from Utah, for five patterns of his design, which he dressed himself.

Tom Mason of Bath, New York, a longtime friend; seven of Tom's patterns, dressed by him personally, appear in the book. Ralph Graves, an outstanding professional tier from Roscoe, New York, on the Beaverkill, for a beautifully tied Gray Fox Variant.

Ellis Hatch of Rochester, New Hampshire. What a name for a fly tier, huh? A true professional, and one of the best ever to put thread to hook. The Ellis Hatch was named for him by me and appears in the Wet Flies chapter.

Dave Klausmeyer, editor of *Fly Tyer* magazine, for his advice, counsel, and support. Tim Fox of The Fly Shop of Redding, California, for a fine selection of flies and fly patterns. Don Wilson of Portsmouth, New Hampshire, for his excellent Northeastern patterns and flies. Jim Warner of Wolfeboro, New Hampshire, for his original pattern, the Winnipesaukee Smelt.

Ian Cameron, outstanding Maine guide, for his excellent fly patterns. Marla Blair, an excellent guide, for the Jailbird and Para-Dorito patterns, and for being such a good friend. Mike Martinek for eight excellent original patterns, superbly tied by himself. Jim Greene of Bethesda, Maryland, for the Waterwisp fly design.

Andy Burk and the gang from the Reno Fly Shop—Rob Anderson, Dave Stanley, Tim Haddon, "Sugar" Keith Tucker, and Bill Ladner—for their excellent patterns and flies. Blue Ribbon Flies of West Yellowstone, Montana, for their contribution of some of their "go-to" flies.

And posthumously: Marvin Goodfriend, who was instrumental in my development as a tier and fisherman. Among many other things, Marv turned me on to the Grannom, which appears in the Wet Flies chapter. Lew Oatman, formerly of Shushan, New York, for his legacy of three beautiful streamer patterns. Art Flick, formerly of Westkill, New York, for the still-effective patterns in his book *Streamside Guide to Naturals and Their Imitations*.

—1—

Anatomy of a Pelt

A Quantitative and Qualitative Study
of a Dry-Fly Cape and Saddle

The cape (neck) used in the study.

Over the years I've seen many articles in various periodicals, and in books as well, about hackle—specifically, dry-fly hackle. All of them were of considerable interest, as they looked at the subject from various perspectives. Now I'd like to add my two cents' worth (two turns' worth?).

My purpose in this exercise is twofold. First, I want to dramatize the quality to be found in pelts that have markings or color variations that classify them as non-typical, or variant. Also, I want to soften the "sticker shock" by demonstrating their value—that is, the amount of hackle per dollar you can obtain from pelts of this quality. The yield is truly remarkable.

CAPE

First, to lay the groundwork, here's what I hand out to my tying students on the subject of hackle from dry-fly capes, or necks, if you prefer:

Quality Attributes—General
1. Very fine, flexible quills that don't split or break when flexed.
2. Stiff, strong barbs, relatively web-free.
3. High barb count; that is, a dense deployment of barbs on the quill. Notice the high barb count and the strength of the barbs.
4. Consistency of barb length, which is what determines size. The technical term is *linear symmetry*.
5. Equal barb length on both sides of the quill. The technical term is *lateral symmetry*.
6. Beautiful coloration, or sheen.

Cape/Neck Attributes—Specific

1. Long "sweet spots," meaning usable quality throughout a large portion of the feather. This series shows how the long sweet spot, or usable length, of a typical feather from the cape enables the dressing of a fly with a single feather. A tying tip: When using a down-eye hook, do your trimming on top, so as to keep the hook eye clear.

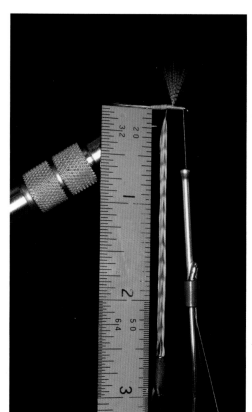

2. Range of sizes. These two photos show a true size 26 hackle. Note that an extra-wide-gape hook is used on very small flies.

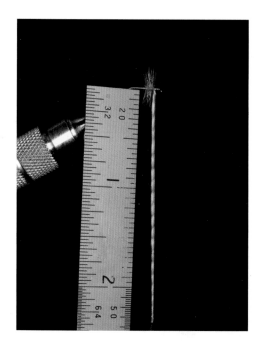
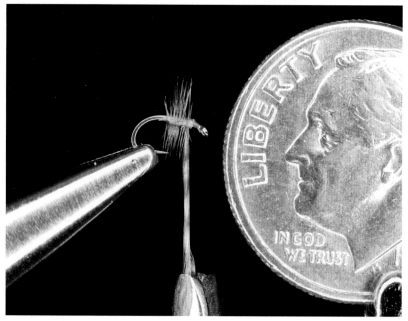

3. Presence of tailing material around the edges of the cape. These are the throat hackles.
4. Bonus: streamer, bugger, and wet-fly hackle at the rear.

For this study, I used a Whiting Farms cape graded silver. As most of you know, Whiting Farms uses what is called an "Olympic" grading system. This means that the pelts are graded gold, silver, and bronze, rather than #1, #2, and #3. (*Note:* On the packages in the shops, the gradings are numeric: 1, 2, 3.) There are also rare and exceptional capes that are graded platinum and ultra-platinum. They are to kill for! But they seldom appear on the shelves of fly shops, so we won't get into them here.

The silver cape I selected would have been a #2 under the numeric rating system. It represents the typical good-quality pelt commonly encountered in shops. I chose it because my intent is to analyze the type of product the average tier is going to buy and use.

As you see, this pelt shows a marked barring. Such pelts are commonly called *variants*. This is due to cross-breeding with the Henry Hoffman strain of grizzly, or barred, rock chickens that Dr. Tom Whiting acquired in 1988. The resultant strain has a very high feather count and features a great many hackles in the smaller sizes. This is quite unique and is not to be found on birds of other lineage.

What I have done is to strip the front portion of the cape, from size 10 down to the tiny stuff at the very front edge. My sizing was based on what has long been considered the norm, which is that the barb length of a feather wrapped onto a standard dry-fly hook will equal one and a half times the gape. *Standard hook* means that the gape is half the length of the shank. Most of the popular brands of hooks—such as Daiichi, Tiemco, and Mustad—adhere to this ratio.

I put the feathers in separate bags and, when finished, counted the number of feathers in each bag. When I got down to the tiny stuff, I applied some additional grading and sizing considerations, as length—meaning usable length—became critical.

First, here's how the count came out for prime feathers. This refers to those taken from the center of the cape and having the longest usable length, or sweet spot:

Size 10	36
Size 12	65
Size 14	67
Size 16	106
Size 18	50
Size 20	35
Size 22	20
Sizes 24, 26, 28	52

Then I bagged and counted those feathers that were not center-cut. Here are the numbers:

Size 12	6
Size 14	13
Size 16	12
Size 18	5
Size 20	10
Size 22	13
Sizes 24, 26, 28	140 (¾ to 1 inch long)
Sizes 24, 26, 28	100 (¾ inch and slightly shorter)

Okay, let's stop there for a moment and go back to the larger feathers. In the size 10 range, the usable length comprised approximately the outer third of the feather. There were a few that were exceptional, in that the sweet spot was long enough to get ten to twelve turns out of a single feather. However, in most cases, one would require two feathers to adequately dress a size 10 dry fly. So realistically, we're looking at a yield of eighteen flies from the centered feathers.

The story on the size 12s was considerably better. Out of a total count of sixty-five feathers, I found that about half of them would yield at least ten turns, meaning that a single feather was sufficient to properly dress a size 12 dry fly. The rest had to be used two per fly. Thus, the total yield was forty-eight flies. The story with the size 14s was almost identical, yielding forty-nine flies.

The Light Cahill Quill in the photographs in this chapter was hackled with a single size 12 feather, using ten turns. As can be seen, this produced a well-packed hackle having uniformity of barb length. In fact, if anything, the fly is slightly overdressed. And by the way, the quill used for the body came from a large feather off the rear part of the cape.

This particular cape was very strong in size 16. Many of these feathers had quite long sweet spots and could easily dress two flies. Even some of the less-than-prime ones might squeeze out a second hackle. However, I wanted to stay on the conservative side, so I've applied the same factoring to the 16s as I did to the 12s and 14s. The result is a yield of 159 flies.

The total numbers in the size 18 category dropped off considerably. This is to be expected, because we're getting into the more narrow part of the cape. However, most of the feathers had remarkably long sweet spots. I was tempted to simply double the count, but again being conservative, I estimated that three-fourths of these feathers would yield two hackles. This makes for a total yield of eighty-seven.

As for sizes 20 and 22, I'm simply doubling the feather count, so the yields are seventy and forty flies, respectively. By the way, this is allowing for slight loss in tying off and tying back on. I'm comfortable with this methodology. Anyone who can't get two generous hackles out of such feathers is being wasteful.

In the case of the smaller feathers, sizes 24 to 28, I'm going back to a one-to-one ratio, simply because the feathers are pretty short, and what's lost in tying off and tying on again would make it unfeasible to try for two hackles. But not to worry—there are so many of them! The centered feathers alone yield fifty-two flies. Another large group that contains feathers from ¾ inch to 1 inch adds another 140 flies.

And what of all those other tiny feathers gathered from around the perimeter of the cape? By sitting at the vise and working with these feathers, I've determined that those with an overall length of ¾ inch or close to it can hackle a tiny fly with no great difficulty. This adds another one hundred flies.

Yes, I lumped together the 24s, 26s, and 28s. The reason is that the difference between the sizes becomes very minimal. Also, if we're judging the size by the barb length relative to the gape of the hook, the design or shape of the hook comes into play. For example, many tiers, myself included, prefer to tie their very small flies on hooks that have a slightly wider gape than the standard size. In other words, the gape is more than half the length of the shank. This enables better hook engagement, and thus more fish brought to net.

I mentioned that there was a group of feathers taken from around the edges of the cape. They totaled seventy-three in all, in various sizes, lengths, and amounts of curvature. These feathers have shorter sweet spots. Also, the barbs on the two sides of the quill are, in some cases, noticeably different in length. But they are not to be discarded! Such feathers make great hackles for Parachute flies, thereby saving prime center-cut feathers for conventional hackles. And as we work toward the outer edges of the cape, we find the so-called spade, or throat, hackles that yield precious tailing material. The amount of these, and the length of the barbs, will vary widely between capes because different strains are interbred to obtain different colors and size ranges.

This still leaves us with a lot of feathers on the cape. I stripped them all from the pelt, discarded those that were of no value, and counted the rest. The total came to 222.

These feathers can be very useful to the versatile tier who ties streamer flies, certain types of saltwater flies, and various types of larger wet flies. Some of them can also be used for big Parachutes, where only the tips of several feathers are used to tie a single fly. There may also be tailing material here, if the tier can work beyond the web line and use just the outer parts of the barbs.

As mentioned earlier, excellent quill bodies may also be fashioned from these large feathers. The quills on this particular pelt are quite flexible and can be wrapped without a lot of splitting. The photographs here of the Light Cahill Quill depict such a body. I do recommend, however, that if you're intending to use these quills this way, they should be stripped ahead of time and stored in a weak mixture of water and any inexpensive hair

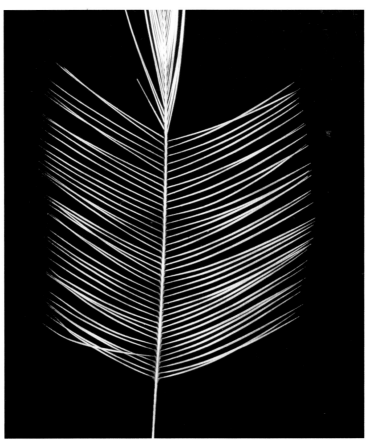

A feather with unequal barb length on either side of the quill makes a perfectly acceptable Parachute hackle.

Larger feathers from the rear portion of the cape can be used to make various types of flies.

conditioner—say 20 to 25 percent conditioner and the rest water. A small, narrow jar is ideal, of the sort spices and olives come in. (I'm a martini drinker, and this affords me an opportunity to recycle the empty olive jars.)

So there's a lot of usable material on a typical good-quality cape. Of course, many tiers buy capes just for the part they use. I know people who tie dry flies in sizes 10 to 14, or perhaps 16, and that's all. It's too bad we can't have a semiannual conclave where everyone brings their partially used capes, and they swap with each other. That's not going to happen, of course, but if you don't tie smaller than, say, a 16, why not cut off the front ends of your capes and donate them to the mini- and micro-fly tiers? They will be eternally grateful.

SADDLE

So what about feathers from the saddles of these birds? There's quite a remarkable story to be told here as well. As with the cape, I stripped this pelt and analyzed the yield. First, I simply removed all of the feathers and grouped them by length. Here are the counts:

10 to 12 inches in length: 336 feathers
8 to 10 inches in length: 84 feathers

These are feathers taken from the sides of the saddle, which is where the best quality is found. I set aside the feathers from the center. Here's the count on them:

10- to 12-inch prime dry fly: 9 feathers

There were also what I call half-and-half feathers. These are soft and webby in the butt section and dry-fly quality from around the middle to the tip. I found twenty of these.

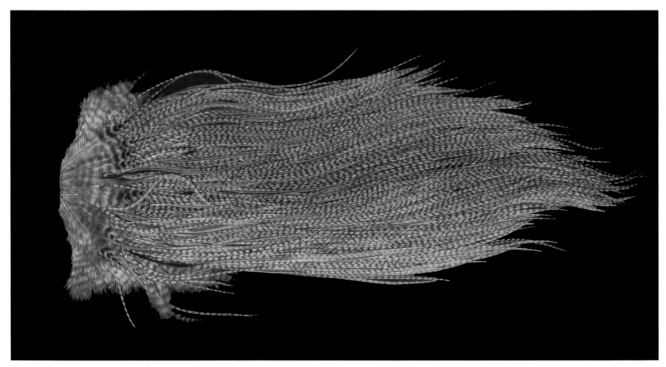

The saddle used in the study.

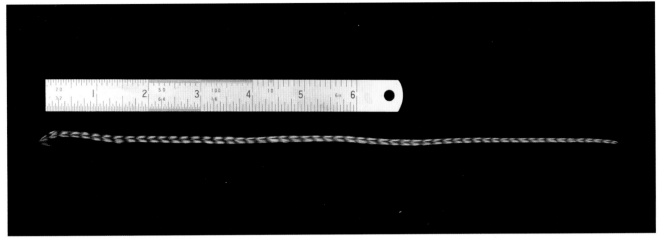

A typical saddle hackle.

There was some schlappen. These are soft, webby feathers that are found just where the tail feathers begin. They're good for making really webby Woolly Buggers and such, if you're so inclined.

Now for the qualitative aspects. Both the 10- to 12-inch and 8- to 10-inch feathers are of superb dry-fly quality, meaning that they have very strong barbs and very high barb counts. They range in size from 12 to 18, a wider range than is typical for saddles. There weren't a lot of 12s and 18s, however. Sizes 14 and 16 predominated.

What's truly remarkable is that there is virtually no waste on these feathers. The dry-fly quality begins almost at the very butt, so you need discard only about ¾ inch, on the average. The quills are thin and flexible, and wrap perfectly. The high barb count means more hackle per turn.

A few of the longest feathers actually have three sizes on them. While I would prefer the barb length to be more uniform, I don't consider this a serious detriment, as I tie in all of those sizes. Also, it's not all that prevalent. Most of the feathers are pretty consistent in barb length.

To demonstrate, I put a large streamer hook in the vise and tied as many

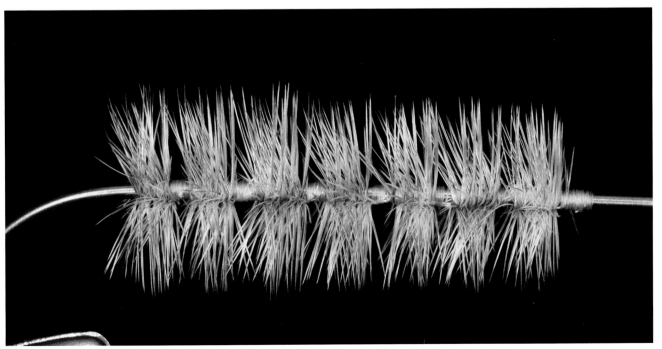

Seven size 16 hackles from one feather.

Wrap the feathers pretty-side forward, so that the barbs don't lean.

simulated hackles as the feather, a size 16, would yield. I took six turns for each hackle, that being quite sufficient to properly dress a dry fly in this size range, with a feather of this quality. In order to accurately determine how many flies could be tied from this feather, I treated it as I would in actual tying, meaning that I tied on and off, stripping sufficient material from the quill for each tie-in. The result, as the photo shows, is seven perfect hackles.

Let's do the math. So as to be ultra-conservative, let's assume four hackles per feather from the 8- to 10-inch and 10- to 12-inch feathers combined. That's 420 feathers times 4, for a yield of 1,680 sets of hackles. I know this sounds like an awful lot, but the numbers don't lie. Now you can see why commercial fly-tying operations opt for pelts in this quality category: The yield is enormous. And this explains how such pelts justify the higher prices they command.

A note or two on judging size. Both the capes and saddles are very heavily feathered. As a consequence, the barbs lie at a very steep angle along the quill. This can be deceptive, as it makes the feathers look as though the hackle barbs are shorter than they actually are. Be sure to fully flex the feathers when judging size.

The very long feathers from the saddles usually run quite consistent in barb length throughout the length of the feather. However, sometimes you'll find more than one size on a feather: for example; size 14s nearest the butt end and size 16s farther out toward the tip end. This is okay, so long as you're aware of it.

A note on wrapping these feathers, both cape and saddle: It's important that the "pretty" side of the feather be facing frontward. This results in the barbs being deployed virtually straight up and down. If the dull side faces the front, the barbs have a tendency to lean forward. This creates difficulty, as succeeding wraps have a tendency to get caught up in the previous ones.

When evaluating saddles, and for that matter capes, make note of the uniformity of barb length on either side of the quill. If it's moderate, no problem. By moderate, I mean no more than a half-size. Significant differences in barb length will result in less-than-ideal hackles.

So what about pelts that you already own? If the differential is no more than one size, go ahead and tie with them. Your hackles may not be as aesthetically pleasing as you might wish, but the flies will fish okay. In cases where barb differential is more extreme, well, just tie Parachute flies with those feathers.

Whiting Farms pelts are truly exceptional. However, I have to mention two other outstanding growers of genetic hackle. They are Bill Keough and Charley Collins. Both raise very good-quality dry-fly birds in a wide range of colors, and they offer excellent value for the money. A good way to find out where their products can be purchased is to google "Keough Hackle" and "Collins Hackle." You'll see a number of sources. I should also mention that both growers have booths at some of the weekend shows on the winter circuit, where you can examine their pelts up close and personal.

Today is May 12, 2007, and I'm tying for my upcoming Montana trip. I just dressed eight size 14 caddis dry flies with one feather from a straw cream Whiting Farms saddle—and with palmered hackles, yet. This stuff is for real, my friends.

— 2 —

Dry Flies

THE ADAMS

I would be remiss if I were to omit the timeless Adams, as it has always been a great pattern, and always will be. I might offer a couple of tying suggestions.

Adams, Hen Wing

A hen cape with light-dark barring and some web in the center makes a better set of tippet wings than does a rooster cape. When tying them in, I don't strip the quills bare, but rather fold back the barbs, exposing the tie-in spot. This makes it much easier to get the wings to go on straight and also contributes to durability.

DRESSING

HOOK: Typical dry fly; here, the Daiichi model 1180; sizes 10 to 16. **THREAD:** Black 8/0 Uni-Thread or similar. **WINGS:** Two tippets from a grizzly hen cape, tied back-to-back. **TAIL:** Hackle barbs; brown or brown and grizzly mixed. **BODY:** Fine, soft medium gray dubbing. **TACKLE:** Brown and grizzly mixed.

TYING STEPS

1. When tying tippet wings, I find it helpful to simply fold back the barbs, exposing the tie-in point, rather than stripping the quills bare. This keeps the quills from rolling and makes for a more stable set of wings.

2. The butt material is simply trimmed and covered with thread.

3. The finished fly.

Adams Light, Teal Wing

The Adams can also be tied with wings of teal flank, as the markings are reasonably similar to those of the grizzly. Here's a light-colored version:

DRESSING

HOOK: Typical dry fly; here, the Daiichi model 1180; sizes 10 to 16. **THREAD:** Tan, beige, or camel 8/0 Uni-Thread or similar. **WINGS:** A barred teal flank feather, tied wood duck–style. **TAIL:** Hackle barbs; light ginger or light ginger and grizzly mixed. **BODY:** Fine, soft medium gray dubbing. **HACKLE:** Light ginger and grizzly mixed.

TYING STEPS

1. The wing is done just like any classic wood duck–wing fly—the Light Cahill, whatever—except that barred teal is used instead.

2. The finished fly.

BIVISIBLES

The extremely simple Bivisible style of fly is still very productive in faster currents and in failing light. These are great "training" flies for the fledgling tier. Dry-fly hackle wrapped from the rear of the hook forward over most of the hook's length is called *palmered* hackle, for some obscure reason. These flies balance better on the water if the body hackle is cut shorter than with conventional dry flies—in other words, about equal to the gape of the hook. Tie it in with the pretty side facing forward, and keep it so when wrapping. Keep the turns tight together, i.e., not spaced.

As the Adams dressing indicates, the basic Bivisible design can be supplemented by the addition of a tail and/or an underbody.

Brown Bivisible

DRESSING

HOOK: Dry fly; Daiichi model 1180 or similar; sizes 10 to 14. **THREAD:** Black 8/0 Uni-Thread or similar. **HACKLE:** Brown, wrapped palmer-style, fronted by white.

Badger Bivisible

DRESSING

HOOK: Dry fly; Daiichi model 1180 or similar; sizes 10 to 14. **THREAD:** Black 8/0 Uni-Thread or similar. **HACKLE:** Badger, wrapped palmer-style, fronted by white.

Adams Bivisible

DRESSING

HOOK: Dry fly; Daiichi model 1180 or similar; sizes 10 to 14. **THREAD:** Black 8/0 Uni-Thread or similar. **TAIL:** Hackle barbs; brown or brown and grizzly mixed. **BODY:** Medium gray dubbing. **HACKLE:** Mixed brown and grizzly, wrapped palmer-style, fronted by white.

WINGED BLACK ANT THAT'S ALMOST TOO EASY

Continuing my romance with closed-cell foam, I've redesigned a fly that's brought me a lot of thrills over the years. Flying ants are an infrequent occurrence, but when such a flight happens, it's a bonanza!

DRESSING

HOOK: Light-wire scud, small; here, the Daiichi model 1130; size 16. **THREAD:** Black 6/0 or 8/0 Uni-Thread or similar. **BODY SECTIONS AND HEAD:** A strip of black closed-cell foam, 1/8 inch in width, rounded at the rear. **WINGS:** Translucent synthetic yarn, such as Antron, Zelon, or Darlon.

TYING STEPS

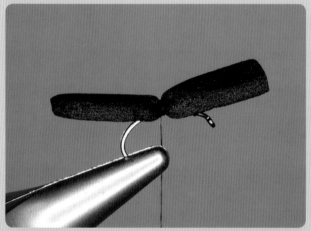

1. Wrap the hook with several layers of thread, then tie on the foam strip in the position shown.

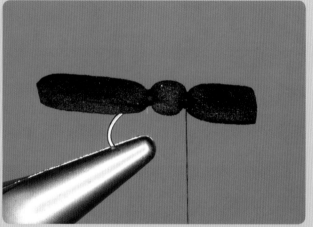

2. Advance the thread and tie down the foam, forming the second body section.

3. Pass the thread underneath the hook and X-wrap the wing material between the rear and second body sections. Advance the thread forward again and tie off. Shape the head, trim the wings to length, and put a small droplet of superglue on the X-wraps that tied on the wing.

BLOODY BUTT CADDIS

This pattern was contributed by Ian Cameron.

IAN'S NOTES

The Bloody Butt Caddis is an excellent all-around brookie fly. They like red! You can tie the head just like a regular Elk Hair Caddis, if you want.

BLUE QUILL

This pattern imitates the mayfly *Paraleptophlebia adoptiva* and a couple of closely related insects. It's tied by Tom Mason.

DRESSING

HOOK: Typical dry fly; Daiichi model 1180 or similar; sizes 16 and 18. **THREAD:** Brown or camel 8/0 Uni-Thread or similar. **WINGS:** Gray hen hackle tippets. **TAIL:** Medium gray dun hackle fibers or Microfibetts of that color. **BODY:** A stripped quill from a peacock herl frond, not from the eyed part. **HACKLE:** Medium gray dun.

TYING NOTES

Quills taken from the non-eyed portion of the peacock tail are darker and have much less light-dark contrast than those taken from the eyed portion.

BLUE-WINGED OLIVE EMERGER

This pattern was contributed and tied by Tom Mason.

CAHILL QUILL

DRESSING

HOOK: Typical dry fly; Daiichi model 1180 or similar; sizes 12 and 14. **THREAD:** Beige or tan 8/0 Uni-Thread or similar. **WINGS:** Wood duck flank. **TAIL:** Cream hackle barbs. **BODY:** A stripped quill from a cream or straw cream cape. **HACKLE:** Cream.

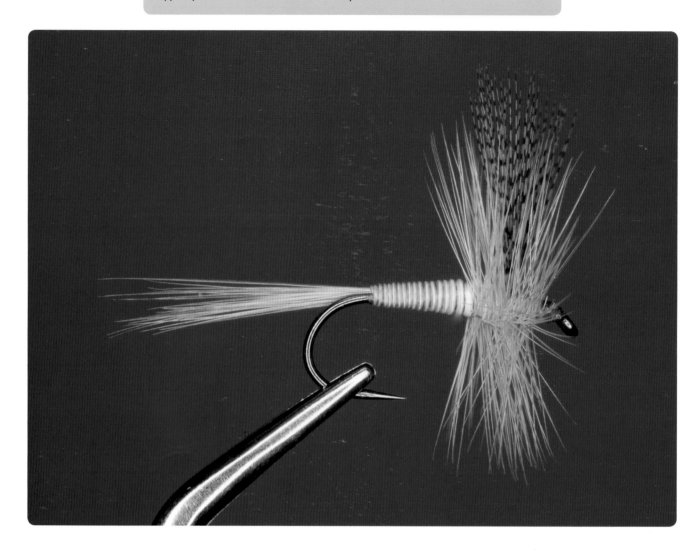

DATUS PROPER PERFECT DUN (CORNUTA)

This is another pattern contributed and tied by Tom Mason.

> **DRESSING**
>
> **HOOK:** Mustad model 94831 1XL or comparable; size 16. **THREAD:** Olive 8/0 Uni-Thread or similar. **WINGS:** Grizzly dyed dun hackle tips, tied extra-long. **TAIL:** Two small bunches of dun hackle barbs, divided. **BODY:** Medium olive dubbing. **HACKLE:** Light gray dun, tied thorax-style.

DORATO HARE'S EARS (DHEs)

My longtime fishing buddy Bill Dorato designed this fly many years ago. It's intended to imitate a newly emerged, buzzing adult caddis striving to leave the water. The bottom of the hackle is clipped off, which facilitates fishing with a "high-sticking" technique, making the fly hop and skip on the water. It's also a very effective "probing" fly for fishing the likely lies when no surface feeding is happening. Until I discovered the Turck's Tarantula, this was the only dry fly I knew of that used hare's ear for the body.

DHE Basic

DRESSING

HOOK: Dry fly; Daiichi model 1180 or similar; sizes 10 to 16. **THREAD:** Camel or brown 8/0 Uni-Thread or similar. **WINGS:** Lemon-barred wood duck flank feather. **TAIL:** Brown or mixed brown and grizzly hackle barbs, tied very short. **BODY:** Gray-brown hare's ear dubbing. **HACKLE:** Grizzly and brown, mixed.

DHE Light

DRESSING

HOOK: Dry fly; Daiichi model 1180 or similar; sizes 10 to 16. **THREAD:** Camel or brown 8/0 Uni-Thread or similar. **WINGS:** Lemon-barred wood duck flank feather. **TAIL:** Straw cream or mixed straw cream and grizzly hackle barbs, tied very short. **BODY:** Light-colored hare's ear dubbing mix. **HACKLE:** Grizzly and straw cream, mixed.

DHE Gray Dun

DRESSING

HOOK: Dry fly; Daiichi model 1180 or similar; sizes 10 to 16. **THREAD:** Camel or brown 8/0 Uni-Thread or similar. **WINGS:** Barred teal or mallard flank feather. **TAIL:** Gray or mixed gray and grizzly hackle barbs, tied very short. **BODY:** Gray hare's ear dubbing mix. **HACKLE:** Grizzly and gray dun, mixed.

GRAY FOX

This is the traditional dressing that goes all the way back to Preston Jennings. We thought all those years that it was a distinct insect named *Stenonema fuscum*. Now DNA has proven it to be just a pale march brown, *S. vicarium*— but the trout couldn't care less.

DRESSING

HOOK: Typical dry fly; Daiichi model 1180 or similar; sizes 10 and 12. **THREAD:** Beige or tan 8/0 Uni-Thread or similar. **WINGS:** Wood duck flank or teal flank. **TAIL:** A mixture of grizzly and straw cream hackle barbs. **BODY:** Beige dubbing. **HACKLE:** A mixture of grizzly and straw cream.

GRAY FOX VARIANT

In 1947 a modest book was published titled *A Streamside Guide to Naturals and Their Imitations*. The author was Art Flick, who lived adjacent to Schoharie Creek most of his life and knew his trout stream like few men have known their own. Three of the flies in the book were called *Variants*. The Variant style of fly is characterized by oversize hackles and the absence of wings.

Art gave us three dressings: the Dun Variant, the Cream Variant, and the Gray Fox Variant. The latter has proven to be a fly of enduring value. Interestingly, Art didn't design it to imitate the former *Stenonema fuscum*. He originally intended it to be an imitation of the eastern green drake, *Ephemera guttulata*, but it turned out to be much more than that. It's still one of the best "probing" flies around, and will bring trout to the surface during periods of inactivity.

The beautiful rendition in the photograph was tied by Ralph Graves, an outstanding fly tier from Roscoe, New York.

DRESSING

HOOK: Dry fly; Daiichi model 1180 or similar; sizes 14 and 16. **THREAD:** Tan, brown, or camel 8/0 Uni-Thread or similar. **TAIL:** Grizzly and ginger hackle barbs, mixed. **BODY:** A stripped quill from a large ginger hackle. **HACKLE:** A mix of three colors—dark ginger, straw cream or light ginger, and grizzly—two or three times the size that would used on conventional dressings for these hook sizes; or, simply barred ginger and grizzly.

TYING NOTES

The main problem in tying this fly is finding hackles large enough, as the genetic hackle growers have concentrated on developing small- to medium-size feathers. Such pelts do exist, however. A good venue in which to look for them is at the numerous fly-fishing shows that go on all winter.

It's a good idea to prepare the quills ahead of time. Strip off the barbs and soak the quills in a mixture of around 20 percent hair conditioner and 80 percent water. This will render them soft and pliable, and they may be stored indefinitely in this mixture.

GREAT RED SPARKLE/CDC SPINNER

This pattern from Thomas Ames imitates the march brown spinner. It will also work for the Isonychia bicolor spinner, commonly called the Leadwing Coachman.

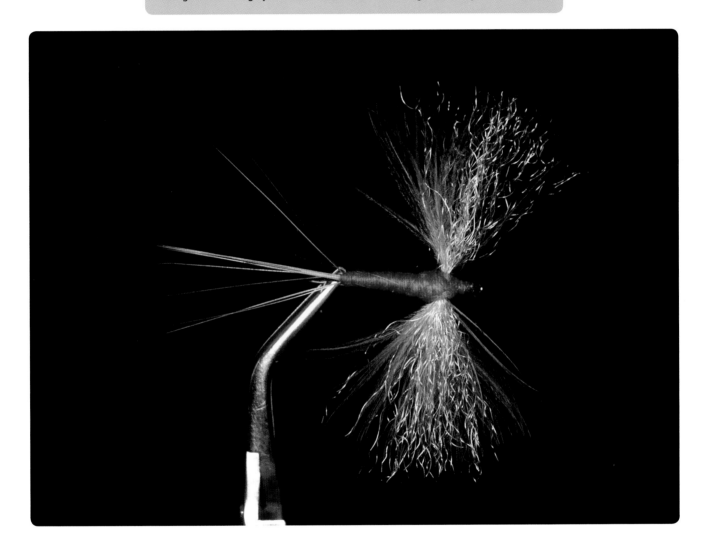

GRIFFITH GNAT

This great all-around mini-fly takes it name from George Griffith, the legendary angler and conservationist of the Michigan Ausable. It seems to produce virtually any time very small insects are on the water.

DRESSING

HOOK: Small, with a wide gape; here, the Daiichi model 1640; size 18 and smaller. **THREAD:** Fine to very fine, black. **BODY:** Peacock herl. **HACKLE:** Grizzly.

TYING NOTES

The long herls found on the back side of peacock sword feathers work very well when this fly is tied in extra-small sizes. If really fine thread is desired, there are several on the market, notably Uni-Caenis and 70-denier Uni-Nylon. Given the availability of Whiting Farms grizzly capes, which are descendants of the Hoffman strain, tiny hackles are not a problem.

HAIR-WINGED CADDIS

This very simple fly has gained great popularity, due in large measure to Montana guide Al Troth, his Elk Hair Caddis, and his highly acclaimed float trips on the Beaverhead. I spent only one day on the river, but it was a most enjoyable one. PMDs came at midday, caddis came later, and the Hair-Winged Caddis worked like a charm.

Basically, there are two versions: hackle and no-hackle. Both elk and deer hair work. The main thing is that the hair should be short, so that the thread intercepts the butt ends when the wing is tied on. It should also be soft, or "pulpy," so that it flares easily at tie-in and floats well. Both the no-hackle and hackle versions of this fly can be tied in whatever sizes and color combinations you need to imitate the caddis you're trying to match.

Tan No-Hackle Hair-Winged Caddis

TYING STEPS

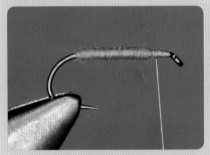 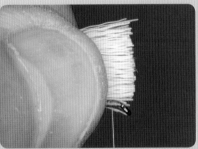 

1. Dub the body and wrap a substantial thread base for the wing near the hook eye.

2. Stack a small bunch of hair and hold it so that the tips extend just a bit beyond the rear of the hook. Trim the hair butts short and square. Hold the hair on top of the hook with the butts extending just barely beyond the eye.

3. Make a series of very firm thread wraps directly on top of each other. The hair butts will flare into a small head. Whip-finish.

DRESSING

HOOK: Typical dry fly; here, the Daiichi model 1180; size 10 and smaller. **THREAD:** Beige or tan 6/0 or 8/0 Uni-Thread or similar. **BODY:** Fine, soft tan or beige dubbing. **WING:** Tan or beige deer or elk hair, as described.

TYING NOTES

Yes, in this case, regular tying thread is adequate for working with hair. This is because of the softness of the hair and the small amount being used. It's important that the head be small but prominent, as it affects at once the image, the flotation, and the behavior of the fly.

Gray-Olive Hair-Winged Caddis

The hackle version is the same as the no-hackle version, with a palmered hackle added.

DRESSING

HOOK: Typical dry fly; here, the Daiichi model 1180; sizes 10 to 18. **THREAD:** Beige or tan 6/0 or 8/0 Uni-Thread or similar. **HACKLE:** Dun or grizzly dyed dun. **BODY:** Fine, soft tan or beige dubbing. **WING:** Deer or elk hair, as described.

TYING NOTES

Keep the hackle short, with the barbs only as long as the gape of the hook. This gives the fly better balance.

HAZEL CREEK

This pattern was contributed by Jeff Curtis of Curtis Wright Outfitters.

DRESSING

HOOK: Dry fly; Daiichi model 1180 or similar; sizes 10 to 14. **THREAD:** Beige or light gray 8/0 Uni-Thread or similar. **WINGS:** Pale watery dun hackles sharply trimmed; refer to the photograph. **TAIL:** Strands of golden pheasant tippet. **BODY:** Pale cream floss or Uni-Stretch. **HACKLE:** Fiery brown and grizzly, mixed.

HENDRICKSON FEMALE DUN

The insect referred to here is the so-called true Hendrickson, *Ephemerella subvaria*. Art Flick, in *Streamside Guide to Naturals and Their Imitations*, described the pattern's color, Hendrickson pink, as the urine-burned fur from the posterior of a vixen red fox—not an easy commodity to come by.

Besides, that was the color of the Hendricksons on Art's home stream, Schoharie Creek. Having fished Hendrickson hatches all over the Northeast and as far west as Michigan, I can tell you that the variation in color is dramatic. I well remember a sunny afternoon on the Willowemoc, the main tributary of the Beaverkill. The female Hendricksons were popping out in good quantity, and they had a rosy cast—almost a lavender. But I noticed that the color faded after a minute or two in the air, and the bodies turned gray.

I guess the message is: Know your local Hendricksons, and if in doubt, use a soft gray color.

DRESSING

HOOK: Typical dry fly; Daiichi model 1180 or similar; sizes 10 and 12. **THREAD:** Gray 8/0 Uni-Thread or similar. **WINGS:** Wood duck flank. **TAIL:** Medium gray dun hackle fibers or Microfibetts of that color. **BODY:** Pink Hendrickson dubbing or a soft gray. **HACKLE:** Medium gray dun.

TYING NOTES

The dubbing I've used here came from a batch I got years ago from a Connecticut dentist named Fred Horvath. He produced a line of dubbing called the Andra Spectrum. This color is very close to what I saw that day on the Willowemoc.

HENDRICKSON MALE DUN, OR RED QUILL

This is the Art Flick pattern from *Streamside Guide*.

HENDRICKSON RF EMERGER

This pattern was contributed and tied by Dave Goulet.

HENRYVILLE SPECIAL

This fly derives its name from Henryville, Pennsylvania, and the Henryville Fly-Fishing Club, which has been the custodian of the Paradise Branch of Brodheads Creek since the late 1800s. It's a general adult caddis imitation—not a very precise one, but quite an effective one—and a pretty fly to boot.

DRESSING

HOOK: Dry fly; Daiichi model 1180 or similar; sizes 10 to 14. **THREAD:** Camel or brown 8/0 Uni-Thread or similar. **BODY:** Green floss or Uni-Stretch. **BODY HACKLE:** Grizzly. **UNDERWING:** A small bunch of lemon-barred wood duck flank feather fibers. **WING:** Two sections (front and back) from left and right gray goose or duck wing quills. **FRONT HACKLE:** Medium brown.

TYING STEPS

1. Wrap the body; it should cover the rear two-thirds of the hook. In the process, tie on the grizzly hackle at the bend.

2. Wrap the grizzly palmer-style, then cut a small groove into the top barbs and lay in the wood duck.

3. Cut the goose/duck wing quill strips and hold them tips-down and with the curvatures flaring away from each other. Tie them on, trim, then wrap the front hackle.

HEN WING DUN (HENDRICKSON, GRAY FOX, QUILL GORDON)

This pattern was contributed and tied by Tom Mason.

DRESSING

HOOK: Daiichi model 1180 or similar; size 12. **THREAD:** Dun gray 8/0 Uni-Thread or similar. **WINGS:** Dark dun hen hackle tips. **TAIL:** Woodchuck tail hair. **BODY:** A light olive/gray goose biot. **HACKLE:** Medium gray dun, tied Catskill-style.

HEN WING SPINNER

This pattern was also contributed and tied by Tom Mason. It's a general spent pattern that works pretty well for a variety of spinners.

DRESSING

HOOK: Daiichi model 1180 or similar; size 14. **THREAD:** Brown 8/0 Uni-Thread or similar. **WINGS:** Light dun hen hackle tippets. **TAIL:** Two small bunches of dun hackle barbs, divided. **BODY:** Rusty spinner; that is, reddish-brown.

CRIPPLED HEX

Large Hexagenia mayflies are present in lakes, ponds, and slower rivers throughout the Northeast and all the way into northern Canada and Labrador. The trout, especially the huge brook trout of Labrador, love to attack the cripples, i.e., the flies that are having trouble casting their nymphal shucks. This is a pattern that I found on the Web site of the Jack Cooper Minipi Camps. (The Web address, by the way, is www.minipicamps.com.) My friend Sim Savage, who has fished the Minipi on six occasions, says this is a must-have for summer fishing there.

This is a wild, hairy-looking fly, so don't worry about trying to be neat. If it comes out too unkempt, just neaten it up with scissors afterwards.

DRESSING

HOOK: Long-shanked dry fly; Daiichi model 2460; sizes 8 to 12. **THREAD:** Brown, camel, or olive 8/0 Uni-Thread or similar. **TAIL:** A short clump of olive-brown marabou. **BODY:** A continuation of the marabou used for the tail or a new bunch, if needed, wrapped. **WING:** A bunch of natural deer hair, tied on top of the hook and leaning out over the eye. **THORAX:** Sparkly dubbing, your choice; here, brown/olive Crawdub from the Spirit River Co. **HACKLE:** Olive-dyed grizzly.

TYING STEPS

1. Tie on the tail and wrap the rest of the marabou for the body.

2. Tie in the wing hair and trim the butts. Keep it on top of the hook and leave a little space at the eye for tying off. Dub the thorax and create a thread base for the hackle.

3. Wrap one or two dry-fly-quality feathers for the hackle and tie them off behind the wing. Then bring the thread ahead of the wing hair, make some wraps to fix it in the leaning-forward position, and tie off.

HI-VIS CADDIS TAN

This pattern was contributed and tied by Dave Goulet.

DRESSING

HOOK: Dry fly; TMC 2488 or similar; size 12 and smaller. **THREAD:** Tan or beige 6/0 or 8/0 Uni-Thread or similar. **RIB:** A thread that matches the overall color of the fly. **BODY:** A dubbing that matches the color of the particular caddis being imitated; here, tan. **UNDERWING:** Pearl Krystal Flash. **WING:** Synthetic Hi-Viz yarn, or if not available, Antron, Zelon, etc. **HACKLE:** Tan or light ginger.

FOAM HUMPY

This pattern was sent to me by Buddy Knight, a guide/tier from Utah. The fly in the photo is one Buddy sent me, and as you can see, his flies are perfectly tied. It's a size 16, which is a good size match for the very common Callibaetis hatches of the West. Buddy says it also works quite well when midges are present.

I have never loved tying Humpies. The foam, which replaces the hair hump, is a major improvement. It's much easier to tie, and much more durable.

DRESSING

HOOK: Typical dry fly; Daiichi model 1180 or similar; size 12 and smaller. **THREAD:** Tan 8/0 Uni-Thread or similar. **TAIL:** Coq de Leon tailing fibers from Whiting Farms. **HUMP:** 1mm-thick closed-cell foam strip, ½ inch in length. **BODY:** Dark tan Superfine dubbing. **HACKLE:** One natural grizzly and one grizzly dyed dun, mixed.

TYING STEPS, PER BUDDY

1. Tie in about eight tailing fibers of the length shown in the photo.
2. Tie in the foam so that it hangs off to the rear.
3. Dub the body to the middle of the hook shank.
4. Tie in and wrap the hackles.

ISONYCHIA BICOLOR COMPARADUN

This fly pattern was also contributed and tied by Dave Goulet.

LITTLE MARRYAT, AKA SULPHUR DUN

This pattern imitates *Ephemerella dorothea*. It's another of the several mayflies commonly called *sulphurs*.

DRESSING

HOOK: Typical dry fly; Daiichi model 1180 or similar; sizes 16 and 18. **THREAD:** Yellow 8/0 Uni-Thread or similar. **WINGS:** Pale gray hen hackle tippets. **TAIL:** Pale cream hackle fibers or Microfibetts of that color. **BODY:** A slightly sulphur-ish yellow dubbing, a shade or so darker than for the Pale Evening Dun. **HACKLE:** Pale cream.

PALE EVENING DUN, AKA SULPHUR DUN

This pattern imitates *Ephemerella invaria*. It's yet another of several mayflies commonly called *sulphurs*. The confusion stems from the rather wide color variations of this insect. In fact, until recently there was a mayfly known as *Ephemerella rotunda*, but by studying the DNA, taxonomists found that it was just another color phase of *invaria*. This pattern will also work for *Epeorus vitreous*, another mayfly commonly called a *sulphur*.

DRESSING

HOOK: Typical dry fly; Daiichi model 1180 or similar; sizes 12 to 16. **THREAD:** Gray or olive 8/0 Uni-Thread or similar. **WINGS:** Gray hen hackle tippets. **TAIL:** Medium gray dun hackle fibers or Microfibetts of that color. **BODY:** A slightly sulphur-ish yellow dubbing. **HACKLE:** Medium gray dun.

QUILL GORDON

This pattern appears in a truly excellent book, *Hatch Guide for New England Streams*, by Thomas Ames. The pattern is a variation by Del Mazza, a very fine tier from upstate New York. I love the diffused effect.

DRESSING

HOOK: Typical dry fly; Daiichi model 1180 or similar; sizes 12 and 14. **THREAD:** Gray or olive 8/0 Uni-Thread or similar. **WINGS:** Wood duck flank. **TAIL:** Medium gray dun or grizzly dyed dun hackle fibers. **BODY:** A stripped quill from the eyed portion of a peacock tail. **HACKLE:** Medium gray or grizzly dyed gray dun.

TYING NOTES

For the tail and hackle, I've used a grizzly dyed dun cape I got from Bill Keogh. The quill is taken from the eyed part of the peacock tail, because when stripped, the quill has a light and dark edge, which simulates the insect's segmentation.

ROB'S LOCO ANT

This pattern was contributed and tied by by Rob Anderson, one of the outstanding fly tier/designers associated with the Reno Fly Shop.

DRESSING

HOOK: Tiemco TMC 760 SP; size 10. **THREAD:** Black Danville Flat Waxed Nylon. **BODY:** Loco Foam, black northern lights. **LEGS:** Black Super Floss.

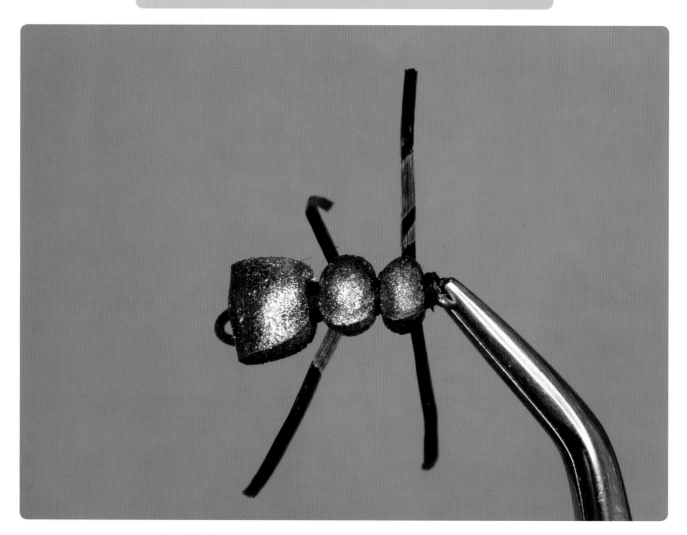

TYING NOTES

The body components are tied using double layers, so that the bottom and top are exactly the same.

ROB'S LOCO HEXAGENIA

The finished fly in photo number 5 was tied by Rob Anderson, the originator. It's a design I've been awaiting for some time. Experience has proven that it's much harder to tie a convincing imitation of a large fly than a small one. That's easy to understand: The fish simply have a much larger image to look at. The Loco Hex is a real breakthrough. It was a struggle for me to learn how to tie it, but well worth the effort. As I write this, I'm twelve days from Labrador and the Minipi, with its giant brook trout and its Hex hatch. This fly is going to get a real workout.

DRESSING

HOOK: Tiemco TMC 5262; size 6. **THREAD:** Yellow Danville Flat Waxed Nylon. **HACKLE POST:** Yellow-dyed elk body hair. **BODY:** Loco Foam, pearl yellow. **RIB:** Yellow Danville Flat Waxed Nylon. **TAILS:** Moose body hair. **HACKLE:** Metz saltwater hackle, yellow-dyed grizzly.

TYING STEPS

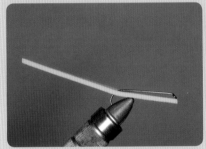

1. Cut a strip of the foam ³⁄₈ inch wide and 2 ½ inches long. De-barb the hook and impale the foam as shown, pearl side down.

2. Hold the foam out of the way and cover the hook with thread. Tie in the wing post, stand it up, and wrap lots of thread around the base. Then tie in the hackle—one or two feathers, as needed—and take some additional wraps around the base of the post, binding the hackle quills into the post so that the feathers stand straight up.

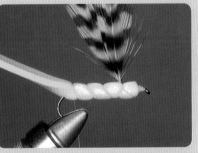

3. Wrap the body segments, folding the foam around the hook.

ROB'S NOTES

This fly is tied commercially by Umpqua Feather Merchants, according to the specifications shown here. Use thread to build up the thorax area, so that it's wider than the body. The body should have four segments on the hook shank and five and a half segments beyond the hook shank, with each segment being slightly smaller, working rearward. The tail should be approximately three-fourths the length of the body.

4. At the last segment before leaving the hook, tie in two moose body hairs on each side of the body.

5. Fold the foam, and while holding the moose hairs along each side of the foam, wrap the extended body segments, rearward and then back forward. Use lift-over wraps to do this. Be sure that the second set of wraps coincides with the first set. Continue over the body segments, tie down and trim off the moose hairs, then wrap the Parachute hackle and tie it off.

AUTHOR'S NOTES

This fly is a bit of a challenge, and some practice is required. However, I assure you that it's worth the effort if you'll be fishing wherever the giant Hexagenia mayflies are hatching. I made a few substitutions, as I didn't have exactly the materials specified. The wing post is plain elk body hair, and the hackle is from Whiting Farms.

As a final note, if you find the moose-hair tailing bothersome, you might consider using stripped brown hackle quills instead, one on each side.

ROB'S LOCO STONE-SALMON FLY

Side view.

Bottom view.

ROYAL WULFF CRIPPLE

Blue Ribbon Flies contributed this pattern and fly.

In addition to the flies sent to me by Blue Ribbon Flies, I want to add the following design. As far as I know, it was originated by Blue Ribbon Flies. It's called the Sparkle Dun because a piece of synthetic yarn is used in place of the traditional tail of hair or hackle barbs. This emulates a dragging nymphal shuck that the emerging insect is struggling to cast off. It's simply deadly on trout that are keying in on cripples.

I've made one change. The original dressing called for a Comparadun-style wing of deer hair. On larger sizes that works okay, but I find it difficult to manage on smaller hooks. Here I'm using Chickabou, a registered trade name of Whiting Farms. This "mini-marabou" material is found at the posterior of certain hen saddles. It's a very good substitute for Cul de Canard (CDC). The frontal photo clearly shows what accounts for its flotation: It's all those tiny, air-catching barbules along the individual barbs.

The Sparkle Dun design can be applied to just about any emerging mayfly. The pattern I picked up originally from Blue Ribbon Flies was an imitation of *Ephemerella infrequens*, commonly called the pale morning dun. This is a very important hatch throughout the Western trout fishery.

DRESSING

HOOK: Dry fly; Daiichi model 1180 or similar; sizes 12 to 20. **THREAD:** Olive 8/0 Uni-Thread or similar. **WING:** An upright clump of pale gray deer hair or Chickabou, as shown here. **TAIL:** A short, sparse strand of tan- or rust-colored synthetic yarn, such as Zelon or Antron. **BODY/THORAX:** Yellowish dubbing; here, PMD Skeeter Fuzz (see tying notes).

Side view.

Front view.

TYING NOTES

Skeeter Fuzz is the generic name for a dubbing that I consider to be the most user-friendly of all the soft, fine-packing dubbings. It also goes by the name of X-Dub at Blue Ribbon Flies and Uncle Dickie's Dubbing at Down 'N Trout Outfitters of Point Pleasant, New Jersey (not my idea, but yes, it was named it after Yours Truly). This is great stuff; it's truly the dubbing for people who hate dubbing. I use it in general tying and especially on really small flies, as it dubs down practically to thread diameter which facilitates figure-eighting a thorax below the hackle on this fly. It is also available on the Web site, www.flytyersdungeon.com.

SPINNERS

In addition to the several insect-specific spinner patterns included in this chapter, I have listed here a small group of general patterns. I've found that if you carry these in several sizes, you'll be prepared for whatever spinner fall may ensue. Of course, there's no substitute for knowing the bugs on the rivers you fish. This will enable you to carry the patterns and sizes for the spinners you expect to encounter.

Rusty Spinner

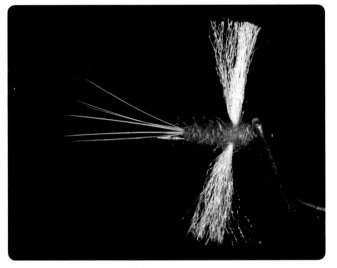

Dark Olive Spinner

DRESSING

HOOK: Typical dry fly; Daiichi model 1180 or similar; sizes 10 to 18. **THREAD:** Rust 8/0 Uni-Thread or similar. **WINGS:** The palest gray or clear synthetic yarn (see tying notes). **TAIL:** A few pale gray or white hackle fibers, or Microfibetts of that color. **BODY/THORAX:** Rusty-colored dubbing.

DRESSING

HOOK: Typical dry fly; Daiichi model 1180 or similar; sizes 10 to 18. **THREAD:** Olive 8/0 Uni-Thread or similar. **WINGS:** The palest gray or clear synthetic yarn (see tying notes). **TAIL:** A few pale gray or white hackle fibers, or Microfibetts of that color. **BODY/THORAX:** Medium to dark olive-colored dubbing.

TYING NOTES

For years I used hackle for my spinner wings, because I didn't like the synthetic yarns of that era. I have now switched to synthetics with the advent of the "On's and Lon's": Antron, Zelon, Darlon, and so forth. They have the requisite texture for making attractive spinner wings that retain their shape fairly well.

For dubbing, use whatever looks good to you and is of a texture that works for the size hook you're tying on. For larger flies using the more sparkly dubbings, the spinning loop technique is recommended. For smaller flies, using soft fine-packing dubbings such as my favorite Skeeter Fuzz, single-thread dubbing works fine.

The tails should be sparse and spread a little. Spreading can be effected by simply wrapping a small ball of thread at the hook bend and jamming the fibers against it. That's why the threads listed are at least close in color to the dubbing.

SPINNERS (continued)

Bright Olive Spinner

HOOK: Typical dry fly; Daiichi model 1180 or similar; sizes 10 to 18. **THREAD:** Olive 8/0 Uni-Thread or similar. **WINGS:** The palest gray or clear synthetic yarn (see tying notes). **TAIL:** A few pale gray or white hackle fibers, or Microfibetts of that color. **BODY/THORAX:** Bright olive-colored dubbing.

Sulphur Spinner

HOOK: Typical dry fly; Daiichi model 1180 or similar; sizes 14 to 20. **THREAD:** Yellow 8/0 Uni-Thread or similar. **WINGS:** Palest gray or clear synthetic yarn (see tying notes). **TAIL:** A few pale gray or white hackle fibers, or Microfibetts of that color. **BODY/THORAX:** Sulphur-yellowish olive-colored dubbing.

THE STIMULATOR

This wonderful pattern is attributed to Randall Kaufman. It is not only an excellent imitator of the western golden stonefly, *Acroneuria californica*, but is also a terrific general pattern that works almost anywhere. Its floating attributes make it a great indicator fly.

DRESSING

HOOK: Long-shanked dry fly; Daiichi models 1280 or 2460 or comparable; sizes 6 to 12.
THREAD: Bright yellow Uni-Stretch or similar, then tan or brown 8/0 Uni-Thread or similar.
TAIL: Deer or elk body hair. **BODY HACKLE:** Grizzly dry-fly-grade saddle feather, tied palmer-style. **BODY:** The bright yellow Uni-Stretch. **WING:** Deer or elk body hair. **THORAX:** Orange dubbing or wrapped material. **FRONT HACKLE:** Grizzly, wrapped over the thorax.

TYING NOTES

The bright yellow Uni-Stretch used in the beginning serves as both tying thread and body material. After wrapping the body, switch to the regular tying thread, so as to avoid building up a lot of bulk. I prefer to keep the body hackle fairly short, about equal to the gape of the hook, and make my front hackle slightly longer—but that's optional.

STIMULATOR, REDUCED (LARGE STONEFLY)

This pattern was contributed and tied by Tom Mason.

DRESSING

HOOK: Daiichi model 1270 or similar; sizes 4 to 10. **THREAD:** Olive 8/0 Uni-Thread or similar.
TAIL: Short coastal deer hair or woodchuck tail hair. **BODY HACKLE:** Grizzly, palmered. **BODY:**
Pale green stretch nylon, Uni-Stretch or similar. **WING:** Moose body or woodchuck tail hair.
FRONT HACKLE: Brown.

STIMULATOR, RUBBER-LEGGED LIME CRYSTAL

The Stimulator has many variations. Here's one that has become very popular. I was unable to find a specific listing of the components, so I've simply gone generic, describing them by what I see in the sample sent by The Fly Shop of Redding, California.

Side view.

Bottom view.

SULPHUR QUILL THORAX DUN

This is another pattern contributed and tied by Tom Mason.

SWT (SHAPED WING THORAX) FLIES

Back in the 1970s I was able to get my hands on a copy of *A Modern Dry Fly Code*, by Vincent C. Marinaro. I was greatly impressed by his analysis of the trout's window and mirror, and by the photographic sequence that showed how the wings entered the trout's field of vision first, appearing as though they were detached from the image in the surface film.

I worked out a fly design based on Marinaro's principles and a method for tying them. Now, three decades later, this is a revisitation. Improved tools, such as my homemade wing burner, and dubbings that are better suited to the thorax technique make these flies pretty easy to dress.

I reserve these unique flies for the most skeptical of trout in the toughest conditions: slow flat water, bright skies. I've been able to hook fish that I'm sure I wouldn't have fooled with conventional flies, and friends with whom I've shared the SWTs have reported similar success. In fact, Nick Lyons, the founder of the house that published this book and that still bears his name, used to requisition SWT PMDs and small Baetis imitations for his trips to O'Dell's Spring Creek, where they often made the difference on the huge brown trout that live there. I was honored.

I show three patterns here, but rest assured that practically any mayfly subimago (dun) can be so imitated. For the show-and-tell, I've chosen the male Hendrickson, with its light reddish-brown body.

SWT Hendrickson

DRESSING

HOOK: Typical dry fly; here, the Daiichi model 1180; sizes 10 to 14.
THREAD: Camel or brown 8/0 Uni-Thread or similar. **WINGS:** Webby gray hen tippets, shaped in a wing burner or trimmed with scissors. **TAIL:** Medium gray hackle barbs. **BODY/THORAX:** Fine, soft light reddish-brown dubbing. **HACKLE:** Medium gray dun.

SWT Flav

This is a Shaped-Wing Thorax version of the "flav" (*Ephemerella flavilinea*), an important western mayfly.

DRESSING

HOOK: Typical dry fly; here, the Daiichi model 1180; sizes 14 and 16. **THREAD:** Olive 8/0 Uni-Thread or similar. **WINGS:** Webby gray hen tippets, shaped in a wing burner or trimmed with scissors. **TAIL:** Medium gray hackle barbs. **BODY/THORAX:** Fine, soft flav-colored dubbing; here, a brand named Skeeter Fuzz (see Sparkle Dun tying notes). **HACKLE:** Medium gray dun.

TYING STEPS

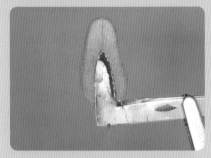

1. Shaping a hen tippet wing in my homemade wing burner.

2. As with all tippet wings (see the Adams sequence), I don't strip the quills bare, but instead fold back the barbs to expose the tie-in spot.

3. The fly is tied in conventional fashion until it's time for the hackle. The hackle is wrapped crisscross-fashion fore and aft of the wings. A narrow worm of the same dubbing used for the body is applied to the thread.

4, 5. A small notch is cut in the bottom of the hackle, and the dubbing is X-wrapped through it, forming a thorax and spreading the hackles into an "outrigger" configuration.

6. The finished fly from the side.

7. A front view.

8. A bottom view.

If you like the traditional stripped brown hackle quill for the body (refer to traditional dressing), you can still tie the fly SWT-style. Simply make the thorax out of a dubbing of compatible color.

THE THUNDERHEAD

This pattern was contributed by Jeff Curtis of Curtis Wright Outfitters.

DRESSING

HOOK: Dry fly; Daiichi model 1180 or similar; sizes 12 to 16. **THREAD:** Black 8/0 Uni-Thread or similar. **WINGS:** White calf tail or calf body hair. **TAIL:** A small, short bunch of brown hair, such as bucktail. **BODY:** Medium gray dubbing, floss, or Uni-Stretch. **HACKLE:** Fiery brown.

A little tip: In the case of down-eye hooks, it's much easier to trim excess materials and keep the hook eye clear by tying off on the top.

TOMMY'S ROUGH RIDER

This pattern and fly were contributed by The Fly Shop of Redding. It bears the name of its originator, Tom Wilson.

DRESSING

HOOK: Typical dry fly; TMC 100 or similar; sizes 12 to 16. **THREAD:** Gray or black Danville Flymaster 6/0 or similar. **TAIL:** Brown and grizzly hackle fibers. **BODY:** Superfine-brand dubbing; tan and Callibaetis colors mixed. **WINGS:** Coastal black-tailed deer hair. **HACKLE:** Brown and grizzly.

TYING NOTES

The fly shown here is the actual example sent by The Fly Shop. I notice that the wings and hackle are quite conservative in length. As for the dubbing, feel free to substitute, providing the color match is close.

TRICOS

Ah, nature's cruel joke on the aging angler! We may hate these miniature mayflies, but the trout love them. During a heavy hatch, they eat them in gulps, like a whale eating krill.

Half and Half Trico

Tricorythodes stygiatus and its relatives have an extremely short life as a subimago, or dun. Often, the spinners are returning to the water while the hatch is still in progress. This innovation represents both phases and comes from Del Bedinotti, a longtime fishing friend.

DRESSING

HOOK: Small, with a wide gape; here, the Daiichi Model 1640; size 20 and smaller. **THREAD:** Fine to very fine, black. **TAIL:** Silvery gray or white hackle barbs, just a small bunch. **BODY/THORAX:** The very finest black dubbing or simply tying thread (see tying notes). **HACKLE/WINGS:** Silvery gray or white, with the bottom barbs removed.

TYING NOTES

Here again, my dubbing of choice is Skeeter Fuzz (see Sparkle Dun tying notes), also called X-Dub at Blue Ribbon Flies. It packs down almost to thread diameter.

Trico Lady Spinner

In flight, the female Trico carries an oversize fertilized egg mass that's a sort of dull green. Thomas Ames, in his wonderful book *Hatch Guide for New England Streams*, refers to it as forest green. I haven't tried to tie an imitation of that, because from what I can tell, the little bug drops the mass while airborne. Thus, the body color of this pattern.

DRESSING

HOOK: Small, with a wide gape; here, the Daiichi Model 1640; sizes 20 and smaller **THREAD:** Olive or green 8/0 Uni-Thread or something even finer. **TAIL:** Silvery gray or white hackle, just a few barbs. **BODY/THORAX:** The very finest subdued green dubbing or simply tying thread. **HACKLE/WINGS:** Clear Zelon or a similar synthetic yarn, tied spent.

THE USUAL

This pattern is attributed to Francis Betters, but I believe it may have actually been the brainchild of his father, perhaps with contributions from others within the tight little group that frequented New York's West Branch of the Ausable River years ago. The story goes that the name of the fly was a by-product of secretiveness. One of the group would hook a trout, and another would call out, "What are you using?" The answer was, "The Usual!" Outsiders could only guess what the Usual exactly was.

This is a very simple fly; however, two of the three components call for hair from the foot of a snowshoe rabbit. This short, coarse material is not easy to work with, but with a bit of practice, it's doable.

I've been reluctant in the past to publicize the pattern, because I was worried that few tiers would have access to snowshoe rabbit feet. However, I now see them in the catalogs. And by the way, Fran Betters told me long ago that the best Usuals were tied with hair from between the toes of a winter-phase female snowshoe rabbit. They don't come so-labeled, so make do with whatever you can get.

DRESSING

HOOK: Dry fly; Daiichi model 1180 or similar; sizes 10 to 16. **THREAD:** Tan, camel, or brown 6/0 or 8/0 Uni-Thread or similar. **TAIL:** A short bunch of hair from the foot of a snowshoe rabbit. **WING:** Same as the tail. **BODY/THORAX:** Rough dubbing; beige, amber, or similar.

TYING STEPS

1. Tie on the wing and tail hairs.

2. With the thread, stand up the wing hairs.

3. With the dubbing, form the body and thorax, using the latter to shore up the wing.

VERMONT HARE'S EAR CADDIS

This pattern was contributed by Ian Cameron.

DRESSING

HOOK: Typical dry fly; here, the Daiichi model 1180; sizes 12 to 20. **THREAD:** Tan, camel, or brown 8/0 Uni-Thread or similar. **RIB:** Pearl Krystal Flash. **BODY:** Hare's ear dubbing. **HACKLE:** Mixed brown and grizzly.

IAN'S NOTES

This fly is very easy to tie, and despite its simplicity, it works quite well. Olive hare's ear is also good. Don't put paste floatant on it; rather, use dessicant powder.

WULFFS

Lee Wulff designed two patterns of what he referred to as his "hair-winged flies" circa 1931. They were to become known as the Gray Wulff and the White Wulff. The prime intent was flotation in rough currents, as he was often fishing the brawling Esopus Creek at that time. Allegedly, Dan Bailey renamed them Wulffs when he and Lee were fishing together in Montana, and he redesigned the traditional Royal Coachman as a Wulff pattern. They have survived the tests of change and time, and are still among the most effective of all dry-fly designs.

Over the years a number of hair-winged patterns have evolved that have expanded the Wulff family. The Ausable Wulff is credited to Francis Betters of New York Ausable fame. The Woodchuck Wulff and Twilight Wulff are Dick Talleur dressings.

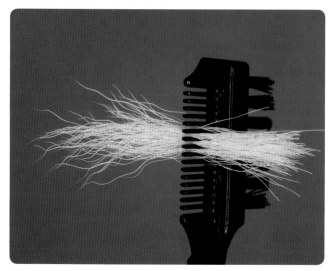

Be conservative; it doesn't take a lot of such hair to make a functional wing. Comb both ends of the bunch—the butts and the tips.

Using a wide-tubed stacker, even up the tips; remove them from the tube facing the way they'll be worked with.

Note: The key to tying good-looking Wulff wings lies in how the hair is handled, specifically calf tail. This is kinky stuff that resists being manicured; hence, the stacking process.

Ausable Wulff

DRESSING

HOOK: Dry fly; Daiichi model 1180 or similar; sizes 10 to 16. **THREAD:** Hot red or orange; here, fire orange 8/0 Uni-Thread. **WINGS:** White calf tail or body hair. **TAIL:** Woodchuck tail hair or moose body hair. **BODY:** Beige or amber dubbing. **HACKLE:** Grizzly and medium brown, mixed.

Grizzly Wulff

DRESSING

HOOK: Dry fly; Daiichi model 1180 or similar; sizes 10 to 16. **THREAD:** First, bright yellow Uni-Stretch, then camel or brown 8/0 Uni-Thread or similar (see tying notes). **WINGS:** Brown calf tail. **TAIL:** Brown elk body hair, to match the wing hair. **BODY:** The bright yellow Uni-Stretch. **HACKLE:** Grizzly and medium brown, mixed.

Royal Wulff

DRESSING

HOOK: Dry fly; Daiichi model 1180 or similar; sizes 10 to 16. **THREAD:** Black 8/0 Uni-Thread or similar. **WINGS:** White calf tail or body hair. **TAIL:** Brown moose or elk body hair, or bucktail. **BODY:** Two clumps of peacock herl, with a center band of Chinese red Uni-Stretch. **HACKLE:** Dark coachman brown.

Twilight Wulff

DRESSING

HOOK: Dry fly; Daiichi model 1180 or similar; sizes 10 to 16. **THREAD:** Black Uni-Stretch, then black 8/0 Uni-Thread or similar (see tying notes). **WINGS:** Black calf tail or body hair. **TAIL:** Black calf tail or body hair, or bucktail. **BODY:** The black Uni-Stretch. **HACKLE:** Grizzly and black, mixed.

White Wulff

DRESSING

HOOK: Dry fly; Daiichi model 1180 or similar; sizes 10 to 16. **THREAD:** Start with white Uni-Stretch mounted in a bobbin; finish with black 8/0 Uni-Thread (see tying notes). **WINGS:** White calf tail or body hair. **TAIL:** White bucktail. **BODY:** The white Uni-Stretch. **HACKLE:** Light badger, aka silver badger.

WULFFS (continued)

Woodchuck Wulff

DRESSING

HOOK: Dry fly; Daiichi model 1180 or similar; sizes 10 to 16. **THREAD:** Camel or tan 8/0 Uni-Thread or similar. **WINGS:** Woodchuck guard hairs. **TAIL:** Light brown elk body hair. **BODY:** Beige or amber dubbing. **HACKLE:** Grizzly and medium brown, mixed.

TYING NOTES

When tying the Grizzly, Twilight, and White Wulffs, I use Uni-Stretch for both the tying thread and the body material. Proceed as follows: Mount the Uni-Stretch in a bobbin and begin by tying in the wing material, but don't stand it up yet. Tie on the tail and wrap the body. Use the Uni-Stretch to make the wing material stand up, then tie it off, tie on the regular thread, configure the wings, and complete the fly.

X CADDIS

This fly was also contributed by Blue Ribbon Flies. It's a cripple pattern designed to imitate emerging caddis that are trapped in their pupal shucks.

DRESSING

HOOK: Dry fly; Daiichi model 1180 or similar; sizes 12 to 16. **THREAD:** Beige or tan 6/0 or 8/0 Uni-Thread or similar. **TAIL:** Strands of gold-colored Zelon, tied as a dragging shuck. **BODY:** Golden-tan dubbing; Antron or natural fur. **WING:** Very fine deer body hair.

TYING NOTES

The wing butts are not completely cut off, but are trimmed short, Elk Hair Caddis–style. Refer to the photo.

YELLOW PALMER

This pattern was contributed by Jeff Curtis of Curtis Wright Outfitters.

DRESSING

HOOK: Dry fly; Daiichi model 1180 or similar; sizes 12 to 16. **THREAD:** Start with yellow Uni-Stretch; finish with yellow 8/0 Uni-Thread or similar. **TAIL:** Brown hair, such as bucktail or elk body hair. **BODY:** The yellow Uni-Stretch. **HACKLE:** Fiery brown and grizzly mixed, palmer-wrapped over the body.

TYING STEPS

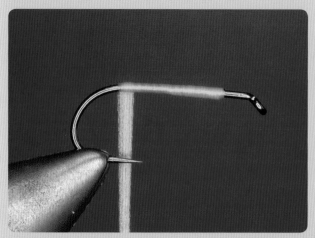

1. Wrap the Uni-Stretch body.

2. Tail tied on, hackles tied in at rear.

3. The finished fly.

TYING NOTES

Mount the Uni-Stretch in a bobbin (see the Tellico Nymph tying steps), tie on the tail, and tie in the two hackle feathers. Then tie off the Uni-Stretch near the eye, tie on with the yellow thread, wrap the hackles one at a time, and finish off the fly.

—3—

Parachute-Style Dry Flies

THE ADAMS, PARACHUTE-STYLE

I love Parachutes, and you'll see lots of them in this book. The Parachute Adams is probably the best known and most popular of all Parachute patterns. It's tied in a wide range of colors and sizes.

Adams Light Parachute

Here's the Parachute version of the light Adams that I find so productive.

> **DRESSING**
>
> **HOOK:** Typical dry fly; here, the Daiichi model 1180; sizes 10 to 16. **THREAD:** Tan, beige, or camel 8/0 Uni-Thread or similar. **WING POST:** A small bunch of white hair; calf tail or body hair, bucktail, or similar. **TAIL:** Hackle barbs; light ginger or light ginger and grizzly mixed. **BODY:** Fine, soft medium gray dubbing. **HACKLE:** Light ginger and grizzly mixed.

TYING STEPS

1. When tying hair-wing posts, I prefer to tie in the hair bunch by the tip ends. This makes a very neat base and helps shape the finished body.

2. Stand up the hair with thread wraps in front, and bring the hairs into a neat bunch by making a few encircling wraps around the base.

3. When tying in the hackle, take a few more encircling wraps around the base and bind the quill of the feather in with the hair. This creates a stiffer base around which to wrap the Parachute hackle. Cut the post to the desired length to finish the fly.

If you prefer a darker Parachute Adams, simply use the dressing listed for the Hen Wing Adams in the Dry Flies chapter, and substitute a hair post and Parachute hackle.

E-FOAM-ERELLA HENDRICKSON SPINNER

A few years ago I was invited to fish at a private club in Pennsylvania. I asked my host what I should plan for in the way of hatches, but he wasn't sure. He told me that general patterns worked fine most of the time, and not to be too concerned about entomology.

As it was early May, I packed fly boxes for what I would expect to encounter on the western Catskill rivers just to the north. This turned out to be the right move. I arrived in the late afternoon, had a quick early dinner, and headed for the river. There, zooming up and down over the water, was as beautiful a flight of egg-laden Hendrickson spinners as I had ever seen. I had some spents with me, and they worked well enough, but I felt that a better imitation would produce more consistently.

And so later that night, the E-Foam-Erella was conceived. I just happened to have some yellow closed-cell foam in my tying kit, and that became the egg sac. It also served to position the split tails perfectly. A Parachute hackle passed for the spent wings.

The new fly worked wonderfully on the club waters and, in fact, everywhere I've used it since. The name, of course, is derived from the Latin name of the true Hendrickson, *Ephemerella subvaria*. I believe the tying methodology is pretty basic, but if further details are needed, they can be found in my earlier book *Inside Fly Tying*.

DRESSING

HOOK: Dry fly; Daiichi model 1180 or similar; sizes 10 and 12. **THREAD:** First yellow, then rusty brown or camel 8/0 Uni-Thread or comparable. **WING POST:** White hair or white closed-cell foam. **EGG SAC:** Yellow closed-cell foam. **TAILS:** Stripped quills, light-colored, very fine, and spread. **BODY/THORAX:** Rusty-colored dubbing. **HACKLE:** Pale gray or white, tied Parachute-style.

TYING NOTES

The yellow thread used in the beginning matches the color of the egg sac. The strip of closed-cell foam is tied down around the bend a little ways, and hanging off to the rear. Then it is folded forward and tied off. At that point the brown thread is swapped for the yellow.

ISONYCHIA PARACHUTE (EARLY AND LATE SEASON)

Tom Mason contributed this dressing and tied the fly.

DRESSING

HOOK: Mustad model 94831 1XL or similar; sizes 14 and 16. **THREAD:** Gray dun 8/0 Uni-Thread or similar. **WINGS:** Dark dun hen tied upright and together to form a post. **TAIL:** Woodchuck tail hair. **BODY:** An olive-dyed quill from the eyed portion of a peacock tail feather. **THORAX:** Dark olive dubbing. **HACKLE:** Medium to dark dun, tied Parachute-style.

THE KLINKHAMER

Hans van Klinken sent this wonderful fly design across the Atlantic from the Netherlands. It is called the Klinkhamer Special or simply the Klinkhamer. It's become a go-to fly for me, and I carry it in several sizes and colors.

A fishing tip: Apply flotant to only the hackle and wing post, so that the body of the fly hangs beneath the surface. A tying tip: Because of the curvature of this hook, you might find it easier to apply the dubbing to the body by repositioning the hook, then restoring it to the starting position once the body is in place.

Here are several of my favorite Klinkhamer dressings.

Klinkhamer Special

DRESSING

(This dressing attempts to closely emulate the original.)
HOOK: Light-wire scud; Daiichi model 1130 or similar; sizes 8 to 18.
THREAD: Gray or tan 8/0 Uni-Thread or similar. **WING POST:** White poly yarn or similar synthetic yarn. **BODY:** Beige/amber synthetic dubbing; Fly-Rite poly 2 #19 or #20 or similar. **THORAX:** Several strands of peacock herl. **HACKLE:** Medium gray dun.

Klinkhamer, Green

DRESSING

HOOK: Light-wire scud; Daiichi model 1130 or similar; sizes 10 to 16.
THREAD: Olive or tan 8/0 Uni-Thread or similar. **WING POST:** White poly yarn or similar synthetic yarn. **BODY:** Bright green sparkly synthetic dubbing. **THORAX:** Black dubbing or a few strands of peacock herl. **HACKLE:** Ginger or barred ginger.

Klinkhamer, Rusty

DRESSING

HOOK: Light-wire scud; Daiichi model 1130 or similar; sizes 10 to 16. **THREAD:** Camel or brown 8/0 Uni-Thread or similar. **WING POST:** White poly yarn or similar synthetic yarn. **BODY:** Bright, sparkly rust-colored synthetic dubbing. **THORAX:** Black dubbing or several strands of peacock herl. **HACKLE:** Fiery brown.

MARCH BROWN PARA-SPINNER

Dave Goulet contributed this dressing and tied the fly.

DRESSING

HOOK: Dry fly; TMC 100 or 101 or similar; sizes 8 to 12. **THREAD:** Uni-Thread 8/0 or similar, color to match the body. **POST:** Yellow closed-cell foam. **TAIL:** Grizzly dyed tan. **RIB:** Brown sewing thread. **BODY:** Tan/brown fur dubbing. **WING (OPTIONAL):** Synthetic yarn—such as Antron, Zelon, etc.—that matches the color of the particular mayfly being imitated. **HACKLE:** Ginger, tied Parachute-style.

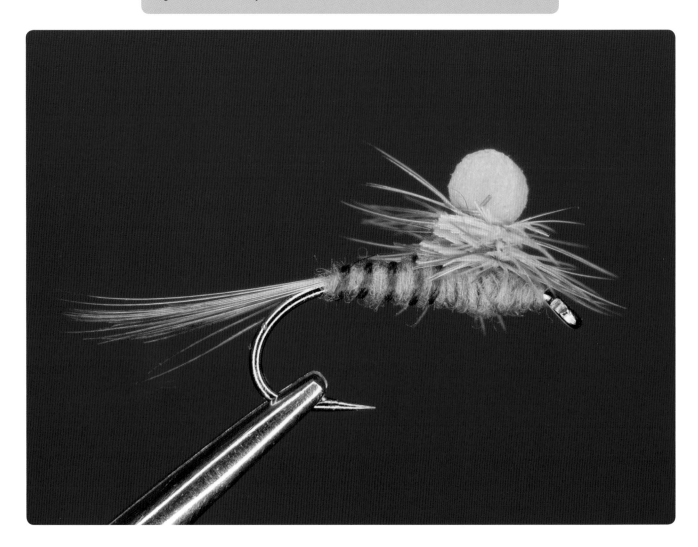

MONITORS

The Monitor style is simply a Parachute that employs a bubble of closed-cell foam for the wing post. I named this modest creation of mine after the legendary Civil Water battleship. They ride low in the surface film, but are good floaters. The foam post makes wrapping Parachute hackle very easy. As with the Waterwisp, many standard dry-fly patterns can be tied Monitor-style. There are a number of closed-cell foam products available. My choice for this application is a product of the Larva Lace Company called Dry Fly Foam.

Monitor, Ginger

> **DRESSING**
>
> **HOOK:** Dry fly; Daiichi model 1180 or similar; sizes 10 and 12. **THREAD:** Tan or camel 8/0 Uni-Thread or similar. **WING POST (BUBBLE):** Closed-cell foam. **TAIL:** Ginger hackle barbs. **BODY:** Ginger dubbing. **HACKLE:** Ginger or ginger-grizzly.

TYING STEPS

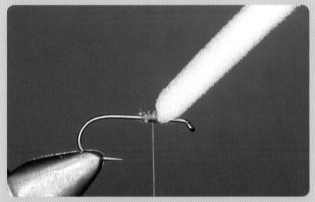

1. The closed-cell foam strip is tied on in this position.

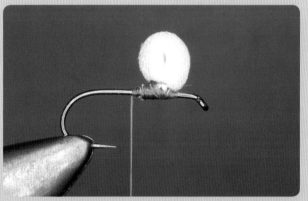

2. The foam is doubled rearward and tied down. The excess is then trimmed off, and five or six turns of thread are wrapped around the base of the bubble.

3. Finish the Monitor as you would a Parachute Adams.

Monitor, Green Drake

See tying steps under Monitor, Ginger.

Monitor, Coffin Fly

See tying steps under Monitor, Ginger.

Top view.

Top view.

DRESSING

HOOK: Dry fly; Daiichi model 1180 or similar; sizes 8 and 10. **THREAD:** Tan or olive 8/0 Uni-Thread or similar. **WING POST (BUBBLE):** Closed-cell foam. **TAILS:** Stripped hackle quills from grizzly neck dyed pale green. **BODY:** Greenish-yellow dubbing. **HACKLE:** Grizzly dyed pale green.

DRESSING

HOOK: Dry fly; Daiichi model 1180 or similar; sizes 8 and 10. **THREAD:** Black 8/0 Uni-Thread or similar. **WING POST (BUBBLE):** Closed-cell foam. **TAILS:** Stripped hackle quills from grizzly neck. **BODY:** White Uni-Stretch or white dubbing. **HACKLE:** Grizzly.

Monitor, March Brown

See tying steps under Monitor, Ginger.

> **DRESSING**
>
> **HOOK:** Dry fly; Daiichi model 1180 or similar; sizes 8 to12. **THREAD:** Camel or brown 8/0 Uni-Thread or similar. **WING POST (BUBBLE):** Closed-cell foam. **TAILS:** Stripped hackle quills from grizzly neck. **RIB:** Thick dark brown thread. **BODY:** Creamish dubbing. **HACKLE:** Grizzly and dark chocolate brown, mixed.

Side view.

Top view.

PARA-EMERGER TAN

This is another pattern and fly contributed by Dave Goulet.

DRESSING

HOOK: Light-wire scud; Daiichi model 1130 or similar; sizes 12 to 16. **THREAD:** Tan or beige 6/0 or 8/0 Uni-Thread or similar. **POST:** Yellow closed-cell foam. **TAIL:** Olive or brown synthetic yarn, such as Antron, Zelon, etc. **RIB:** Brown cotton size A sewing thread. **BODY:** Tan/brown fur dubbing. **HACKLE:** Parachute, color to match that of fly being tied.

PT (PHEASANT TAIL) FOAM EMERGER

This fly is a low-floating replica of the Bottom Feeders, which are covered in the nymphs chapter. A ball or bubble of closed-cell foam takes the place of the bead, and a Parachute dry-fly hackle is added. Similar components are used on the Monitors, and the materials and construction are much the same as that of the Bottom Feeders. However, a light-wire hook is used, and the ribbing wire should be the thinnest available or eliminated entirely. If you have trouble finding ultra-thin copper wire, get a 6-inch piece of stranded speaker wire and remove the insulation. It doesn't get any thinner than that.

> **DRESSING**
>
> **HOOK:** Light-wire nymph/scud; Daiichi model 1150 or similar; sizes 10 to 18. **THREAD:** Brown or camel 8/0 Uni-Thread or similar. **WING POST:** A strip of closed-cell foam, doubled over itself. **UNDERBODY (OPTIONAL):** Brown Uni-Stretch. **TAIL/BODY:** Cock ringneck tail fibers. **RIB:** The finest copper wire. **HACKLE:** Medium gray dun, tied Parachute-style.

TYING STEPS

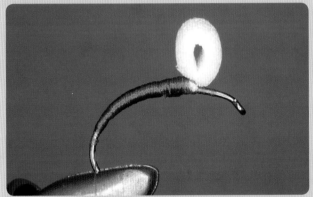

1. When tying in the foam, fold it without crushing it, so as not to collapse the little air bubbles. After securing it and trimming off the excess, take four or five wraps of thread around the base of the bubble, working counterclockwise looking down from the top—unless you tie left-handed, in which case the wraps are taken clockwise. If you're building an underbody, do so now.

2. When tying in the tail, body, and rib materials, you may find it easier to reposition the hook temporarily.

3. Restore the hook to the normal position and configure the tail, body, and rib as shown for the Bottom Feeder. Finish the fly by wrapping and tying off the Parachute hackle. Here again, you'll be working counterclockwise looking down from the top, or clockwise if you tie left-handed.

WATERWISPS

The Waterwisp style of fly rides with the hook positioned up and out of the water. This is facilitated by the unique hook design shown here. Many standard dry-fly patterns can be tied as Waterwisps. The hooks may be obtained from the Web site www.waterwisp.com.

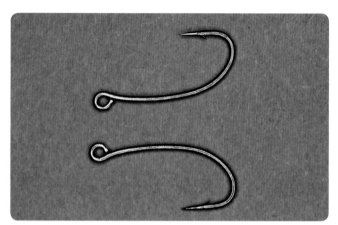

Waterwisp Light Cahill

DRESSING

HOOK: Waterwisp hook; sizes 12 to 14. **THREAD:** Beige, yellow, or tan 8/0 Uni-Thread or similar. **WING:** A small, upright clump of blonde hair. **HACKLE:** One cream or straw cream dry-fly-grade feather. **TAILS:** A small bunch of cream or straw cream hackle barbs. **BODY:** Cream-colored dubbing.

TYING STEPS

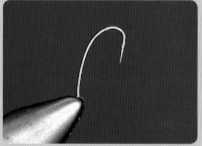

1. The starting position of the hook in the vise. The vise is set at approximately a 45-degree angle.

2. The wing hair and the hackle feather are tied in extending to the right.

3. Rotate the vise 180 degrees, and the hook will automatically be positioned for tying the rest of the fly.

4. Add the tailing bunch and dub the body, finishing with the thread located at the bottom of the hook bend.

5. Wrap the hackle Parachute-style, dull side down, working down the hook bend.

6. A horizontal whip finish is applied, finishing the fly.

WATERWISPS (continued)

Waterwisp Rusty Spinner

See tying steps under Waterwisp Light Cahill.

Side view.

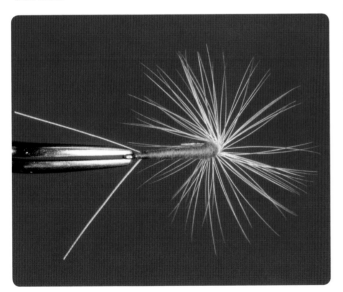

Bottom view.

DRESSING

HOOK: Waterwisp hook; sizes 12 to 14. **THREAD:** Camel or brown 8/0 Uni-Thread or similar. **WINGS:** None. **TAILS:** Very thin stripped hackle quill, white or silver gray. **BODY:** Rust-colored dubbing. **HACKLE:** The palest silvery gray or white.

Waterwisp PMD

DRESSING

HOOK: Waterwisp hook; sizes 14 to 16. **THREAD:** Camel or olive 8/0 Uni-Thread or similar. **WINGS:** Two hen hackles, shaped with a wing burner, or a single upright clump of gray hair. **HACKLE:** Medium gray dun. **TAILS:** A small bunch of medium gray dun hackle barbs. **BODY:** Olive-colored dubbing.

Waterwisp Adams

DRESSING

HOOK: Waterwisp hook. **THREAD:** Black 8/0 Uni-Thread or similar. **WING POST:** A clump of barbs from a barred teal flank feather. **HACKLE:** Brown and grizzly mixed. **TAILS:** Hackle barbs, brown or brown and grizzly mixed. **BODY:** Medium gray dubbing.

—4—
Wet Flies

I began my fly-fishing career as a wet-fly man. I still fish a few traditional wet-fly patterns that I show in this chapter because I love them, and they still work.

Also shown here are a number of what are called Soft-Hackle (S-H) wet flies. These simple little flies have been around almost as long as fly fishing itself, and have been popular on the British chalk streams for centuries. Several of the patterns in Dame Juliana Berner's classic *A Treatise Of Fysshing with an Angle*, which has been around for about 550 years, bear close similarity to today's Soft-Hackle wet flies. There are hundreds of patterns—maybe more than a thousand—and entire books have been devoted to them. Overkill, maybe? Herein, I'll describe just a few that I carry, then you're on your own.

A note of caution: Be conservative with the hackles on Soft-Hackles. The feathers used on them are usually webby, and it's easy to overdress these flies.

CADDIS GREEN S-H

DRESSING

HOOK: Wet fly or scud; here, the Daiichi model 1150; sizes 10 to 18. **THREAD:** Green or olive 8/0 Uni-Thread or similar. **BODY:** Quick Descent dubbing, caddis green (a product of Hareline Dubbing, Inc.). **HACKLE:** A small, tan-mottled Hungarian partridge neck feather.

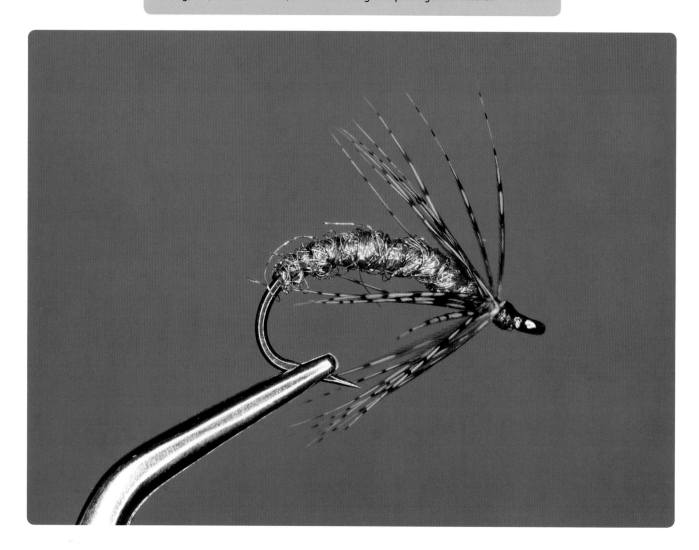

CLARET-SILVER S-H

There's a story associated with this fly. It was the late 1980s, and I was cruising around Montana. I had booked a day on Armstrong Spring Creek in late September. When I stepped out of the motel that morning, I found myself in the midst of a driving snowstorm, with about 4 inches already on the ground. I grabbed a coffee, then drove out to the stream. The snow seemed to be coming down even harder. I was very depressed.

I went back into Livingston and dawdled over breakfast. At 9:00 a.m. one of the local fly shops opened, and I went there to commiserate. The young man behind the counter told me not to lose hope, that the snow was supposed to let up very shortly and it was supposed to get warmer.

Thus encouraged, I went back to the stream. The wind had died down, and the sky was much lighter. A man was standing in the water. Suddenly, there was a rise—and then another. I quickly got into my waders. By the time I reached the bank, the guy upstream was playing a fish. Steady rises followed, and I could see large, gangly Diptera-type flies in the air.

A half-dozen flies later, I was scratching my head in frustration. I hadn't as much as scraped a lip, and the guy above me was hooking up with maddening regularity. Finally, I did something I rarely do: I approached the man and asked him what he was using.

He turned out to be a good Samaritan. He not only showed me his fly, he gave me one. This was truly a blessing, as I had nothing similar.

And so my day was saved. I started taking trout, and as predicted, the weather improved dramatically. By late morning, the sun was out, and small Baetis mayflies were coming off. I put the stranger's fly in a safe place, to be copied later. Here's the pattern.

DRESSING

HOOK: Swimming nymph; Daiichi model 1770 or similar; sizes 10 to 16. **THREAD:** Purple or black 8/0 Uni-Thread or similar. **RIB:** Very fine silver wire, reverse-wrapped. **BODY:** Fine, soft claret dubbing; here, Skeeter Fuzz, my all-time favorite. **HACKLE:** Pale gray Cul de Canard (CDC) or Whiting Farms Chickabou.

BT S-H FLIES

The performance of many Soft-Hackle wet flies has been enhanced by the addition of a bead. Beadheads have gained great popularity, and rightly so. However, I like to place the bead rearward of the hackle. This helps keep the soft feather in position, so that it can undulate enticingly in the currents. I call these flies BTs, for *bead thorax*.

Copper-Pheasant BT S-H

DRESSING

HOOK: Nymph/wet fly; 1XL Daiichi model 1560 or similar, to accommodate the bead; sizes 10 to 16. **HEAD:** A copper bead, appropriately sized for the hook. **THREAD:** Camel or brown 8/0 Uni-Thread or similar. **TAIL (OPTIONAL):** The tips of the pheasant tail fibers that will form the body. **RIB:** Very fine copper wire, reverse-wrapped. **BODY:** A small bunch of cock ringneck pheasant tail fibers. **HACKLE:** Hungarian partridge.

TYING NOTES

Mount the bead by inserting the hook point into the smaller of the two apertures, so that the larger one ends up facing to the rear. Thus, given adroit wrapping of the thread, the bead will hide the finishing wraps. I like to tie back on at the eye of the hook and build a little dam of thread, thus jam-fitting the bead in position.

Gold-Olive Pheasant BT S-H

DRESSING

HOOK: Nymph/wet fly; 1XL Daiichi model 1560 or similar, to accommodate the bead; sizes 10 to 16. **HEAD:** A gold bead, appropriately sized for the hook (see tying notes under **Copper-Pheasant BT S-H**). **THREAD:** Camel or olive 8/0 Uni-Thread or similar. **RIB:** Very fine gold wire, reverse-wrapped. **BODY:** A small bunch of olive-dyed cock ringneck pheasant tail fibers. **HACKLE:** An olive-dyed Brahma hen saddle feather.

Gold-Ribbed Hare's Ear BT S-H

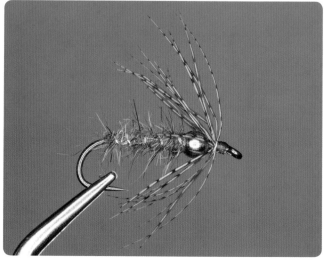

DRESSING

HOOK: Nymph/wet fly; 1XL Daiichi model 1560 or similar, to accommodate the bead; sizes 10 to 16. **HEAD:** A gold bead, appropriately sized for the hook (see tying notes under **Copper-Pheasant BT S-H**). **THREAD:** Camel or olive 8/0 Uni-Thread or similar. **RIB:** Very fine gold wire, reverse-wrapped. **BODY:** Hare's ear dubbing. **HACKLE:** An olive-dyed Brahma hen saddle feather.

GOLDEN BROWN S-H

DRESSING

HOOK: Wet fly or scud; here, the Daiichi model 1150; sizes 10 to 16. **THREAD:** Tan or camel 8/0 Uni-Thread or similar. **BODY:** Ice Dub Golden Brown (product of Hareline Dubbing, Inc.).
HACKLE: Whiting Farms Brahma saddle feather, dyed golden brown or golden olive.

TYING NOTES

If you don't happen to have a Brahma saddle pelt dyed golden brown or golden olive, use a tan-mottled Hungarian partridge neck feather.

THE ELLIS HATCH

I was given this pattern by Ellis Hatch (an unintended pun!) of Rochester, New Hampshire. And he does it justice: He's one of the best ever to put thread to hook. The fly had not been given a name, so I named it after its originator.

DRESSING

HOOK: Nymph/wet fly; 1XL Daiichi model 1560 or similar; sizes 10 to 18, to accommodate the bead, if desired. **THREAD:** Black 8/0 Uni-Thread or similar. **TAIL (OPTIONAL):** A few barbs from a gray-phase Hungarian partridge feather, or none. **BODY:** A stripped quill from the "eye" portion of a peacock tail plume. **THORAX:** A ball of black dubbing. **HACKLE:** A gray-phase Hungarian partridge feather; no more than two turns.

TYING NOTES

I also tie this fly with a black or charcoal gray bead for the thorax instead of the dubbing shown in the photo.

ORANGE FISH HAWK

DRESSING

HOOK: Typical wet fly; Daiichi model 1550 or similar; sizes 10 to 16. **THREAD:** Start with something light in color; finish with black. **TAG/RIB:** Narrow flat gold tinsel. **BODY:** Bright orange floss. **HACKLE:** Light badger.

THREE WINGED WET FLIES

I began my fly-fishing career in the Catskills, on such streams as the Esopus, the Beaverkill, the two branches of the Delaware, and the Schoharie. My mentors were rather wet-fly-oriented. I was informed that above all others, there were three flies that mattered: the Leadwing Coachman, the Hare's Ear, and the Dark Cahill. We fished them two at a time—sometimes all three at once—on droppers. If the trout showed a preference for one of the patterns, we'd switch and fish three of that one. I remember catching triples of the fractious little native rainbows on Esopus Creek.

With the advent of the fly-fishing renaissance after World War II, the traditional wet flies began to be replaced by more sophisticated patterns: nymphs, emergers, that sort of stuff. This was good, and I was very much into it. But to this day, I love to swing a cast of two or three wet flies around in the currents. It brings back memories—and they still work surprisingly well. Maybe it's because so few people fish them these days.

Anyway, here are the basic three. It should be noted that there are a number of variations to each of them. These are the dressings I prefer.

Leadwinged Coachman

DRESSING

HOOK: 1XL wet fly or standard shank; here, the Daiichi model 1550; sizes 10 to 14. **THREAD:** Black 8/0 Uni-Thread or similar. **TAG:** Flat gold tinsel. **BODY:** Peacock herl. **HACKLE:** A rich brown shade. **WINGS:** Gray sections from a duck or goose wing, cupped sides facing inward.

Plain Hare's Ear

DRESSING

HOOK: 1XL wet fly or standard shank; here, the Daiichi model 1550; sizes 10 to 16. **THREAD:** Camel or brown 8/0 Uni-Thread or similar. **TAIL:** A short bunch of Hungarian partridge fibers. **BODY:** Hare's ear dubbing, tied rough. **HACKLE:** Hungarian partridge fibers. **WINGS:** Gray sections from a duck or goose wing, cupped sides facing inward.

THREE WINGED WET FLIES (continued)

Dark Cahill

ONE MORE WINGED WET FLY: THE GRANNOM

I was turned on to this pattern by Marv Goodfriend, a subsequent mentor who had learned that there was more to fly fishing than the basic three wet flies. This is an old pattern that's used to imitate a particular phenomenon: the subsurface diving of the egg-depositing grannom caddis. The tip-off is when you see great flights of these bugs headed upstream. They instinctively know that in order to produce next year's hatch, they must compensate for the downstream drifting that happened during their underwater stages and emergence. Smart little bugs!

DRESSING

HOOK: 1XL wet fly; here, the Daiichi model 1560; sizes 10 to 16. **THREAD:** Tan or camel 8/0 Uni-Thread or similar. **EGG SAC:** Pea green dubbing or one turn of fine pea green chenille. **BODY:** Tan or very light brown dubbing or fine yarn. **HACKLE:** A light brown soft hen feather or a tan-mottled Hungarian partridge neck feather. **WINGS:** Mottled turkey.

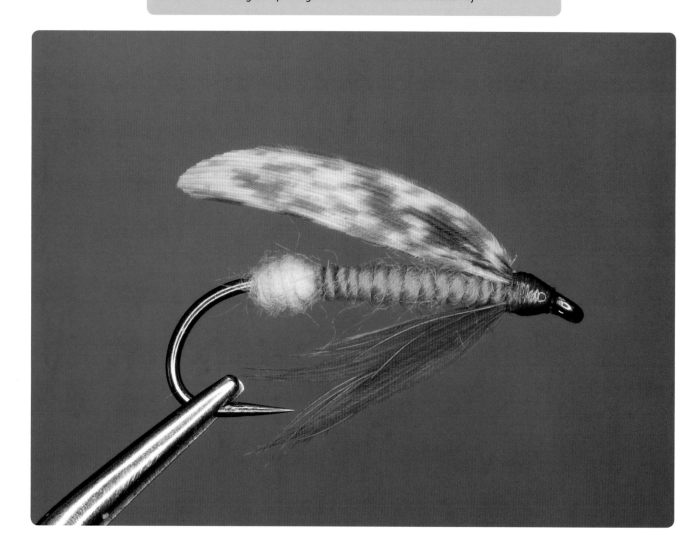

5

Nymphs and Emergers and Such

This chapter contains nymphs and certain other subsurface flies, such as shrimps or scuds and sunken emerger patterns.

AFTERSHAFT NYMPH

Take a look at Gartside's Sparrow in the Special and Novel Patterns chapter, and you'll see a feather called the *aftershaft*. I've used it on this nymph, as it yields a great-looking gilling effect. The large mayfly nymphs of the Ephemera and Hexagenia families are burrowers, and they live in the silt and detritus on the streambed. They need oversize gills to extract oxygen from the water in such surroundings.

DRESSING

HOOK: Longer nymph; here, the Daiichi model 1750; size 8. **THREAD:** Tan or camel 8/0 Uni-Thread or similar. **TAIL:** Short, webby barbs from a speckled hen pelt, or Hungarian partridge. **UNDERBODY:** Weighting wire, 20 to 30 thousandths of an inch thick. **SHELL/WING CASE:** Mottled brown Bugskin. **RIB:** Very fine monofilament. **GILLS:** An aftershaft feather. **BODY/THORAX:** Beige to light brown dubbing. **LEGS:** Same as the tail material.

TYING STEPS

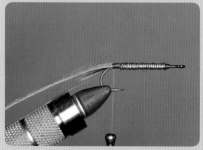

1. Tie on the tail, then tie in the Bugskin upside-down and hanging to the rear, tie in the ribbing mono, and wrap the weighting wire.

2. Tie in the aftershaft feather as was done with the Bugskin, upside-down and hanging to the rear, then dub the body.

3. Bring the aftershaft feather forward over the body, do the same with the Bugskin, and form the segmentation with the ribbing mono, carefully working it between the fibers of the aftershaft feather.

4. Tie in another piece of Bugskin, also upside-down and hanging to the rear. Then dub the thorax and tie on a couple of small bunches of the speckled hen for the legs. Then bring the Bugskin over the top, forming the wing case, and tie off.

5. Aftershaft Nymph, top view.

BIGHORN SHRIMP

This is one of those patterns for which I have no explanation, other than the assurance that it catches trout like mad. It was handed to me during a float down the Bighorn—I think on the same trip where I first became familiar with the San Juan Worm. I was skeptical, but when a master guide like George Kelly turns you on to his go-to fly, you don't ask questions.

DRESSING

HOOK: Typical nymph/scud hook; Daiichi model 1150 or similar; sizes 10 to 14. **THREAD:** Something hot; here, fire orange 8/0 Uni-Thread. **SHELL:** A narrow (⅛ inch) strip of a transparent synthetic material. **RIB:** Fine monofilament, such as 6X or 7X tippet material. **BODY:** A hot blend of synthetic dubbings, of which there are many.

TYING NOTES

There are several clear plastic materials that will serve for the shell. I like Wapsi's Thin Skin, because it comes on a backing, which makes it easy to work with when cutting strips to width. As for the dubbing blend, I'll leave that up to you. To do otherwise would be inappropriate, as I can't try them all. Here, I used a blend of Spirit River's Pseudo Seal, equal parts red and fluorescent orange. For mixing, I use a coffee mill with blades on the top.

BLUE A.P. EMERGER

Buddy Knight sent me this handsome fly. He writes that it's a variation of the Denny Rickards A.P. Emerger, and is one of the most effective still-water patterns he's ever used.

DRESSING

HOOK: 2XL nymph; Daiichi model 1710 or similar; size 12. **THREAD:** Black 8/0 Uni-Thread or similar. **TAIL:** Barred wood duck. **RIB:** Fine dark copper wire. **ABDOMEN:** Blue Superfine dubbing. **THORAX:** Peacock herl. **HACKLE:** Hungarian partridge.

TYING STEPS, PER BUDDY

1. Tie in the tail, the same length as the hook shank.
2. Tie in the ribbing wire.
3. Dub the abdomen to about the halfway spot on the hook shank.
4. Tie in three peacock herls; wrap them forward, then back, then forward again, and tie them down.
5. Wrap the rib, spacing the turns $1/16$ inch apart, over the abdomen and thorax.
6. Tie in four peacock herls, wrap them forward, and tie them off.
7. Tie in the partridge feather by the tip and make one or two turns, then tie off.

BOTTOM FEEDERS

Bottom Feeder flies are, essentially, weighted emergers. The materials and construction are quite similar to that of the PTBT Nymph. However, the curved hook and other components make this fly unique. My intent with this design is to emulate the very beginning stages of an emerging form of life, as the insect prepares to head for the surface.

The Bottom Feeder is as much a design as a pattern. Feel free to innovate. For example, if you'd prefer a dubbed body . . . why not?

DRESSING

HOOK: Typical nymph/scud hook; Daiichi model 1150 or similar; sizes 10 to 16. **THREAD:** Brown or camel 8/0 Uni-Thread or similar. **HEAD:** A copper bead, sized in proportion to the hook. **UNDERBODY (OPTIONAL):** Brown Uni-Stretch. **TAIL/BODY:** Cock ringneck tail fibers. **RIB:** Fine copper wire. **LEGS:** A small dark brown soft hackle feather, one or two turns only.

TYING STEPS

1. Build an underbody with the Uni-Stretch, or not, depending on the hook size and desired silhouette. Then tie the tail, body, and rib, the same as with the PTBT Nymph. Leave space behind the bead for the hackle.

2. Finish the fly by wrapping and tying off the hackle. Move the bead over the thread wraps, then tie on again in front of the bead and wrap a small "dam" of thread, jam-fitting the bead in place.

Olive Bottom Feeder

DRESSING

HOOK: Typical nymph/scud hook; Daiichi model 1150 or similar; sizes 10 to 16. **THREAD:** Olive or camel 8/0 Uni-Thread or similar. **HEAD:** A gold bead; sized in proportion to the hook. **UNDERBODY (OPTIONAL):** Olive Uni-Stretch. **TAIL/BODY:** Cock ringneck tail fibers, dyed olive. **RIB:** Fine gold wire. **EMERGING WING:** A small tuft of gray Chickabou (chicken marabou from Whiting Farms) or regular marabou.

TYING NOTES

Everything is the same as for the basic Bottom Feeder, except that the emerging wing is substituted for the hackle. Note that Chickabou is a registered trade name of Whiting Farms.

BURK'S BOTTOM ROLLERS

I was first attracted to these flies when perusing The Fly Shop of Redding online catalog. There, they are listed as Burk's Czech Nymphs. Andy Burk, the originator, informs me that they're actually Burk's Bottom Rollers. Andy is an outstanding fly tier/designer and guide who works out of the Reno Fly Shop. He tied the flies pictured here, and the specifications are his.

As stated in the preface, substituting materials is a major part of modern fly tying. However, any substitutions in flies like the Burk's Bottom Rollers must be done with great circumspection and attention to maintaining the integrity of the fly's appearance.

Burk's Bottom Roller Psycho Rycho

Psycho Rycho refers to the Ryacophila caddis, this being an imitation of its larval form.

DRESSING

HOOK: TMC 2457 or similar; sizes 8 to 14. **THREAD:** Light olive Danville Flymaster 6/0 or similar. **BEAD:** Black tungsten, 3.3mm for sizes 8 and 10 hooks, 2.8mm for sizes 12 and 14. **WEIGHT:** .020 weighting wire. **RIB:** 5X monofilament, plain or fluorocarbon. **CARAPACE (SHELL):** A strip of Mother of Pearl Sili Skin, tinted with olive and brown Sharpie markers. **ABDOMEN:** Dave Whitlock's SLF dubbing, olive damsel. **COLLAR:** Arizona Synthetic Peacock dubbing, brown.

Burk's Bottom Roller Hare's Ear Special

DRESSING

HOOK: TMC 2457 or similar; sizes 8 to 14. **THREAD:** Tan Ultra Thread, 70-denier. **BEAD:** Gold tungsten, 3.3mm for sizes 8 and 10 hooks, 2.8mm for sizes 12 and 14. **WEIGHT:** .025 weighting wire. **RIB:** 5X monofilament, plain or fluorocarbon. **CARAPACE (SHELL):** A strip of Mother of Pearl Sili Skin, tinted with a gold Sharpie marker over the body and a brown Sharpie marker at the front. **ABDOMEN:** Arizona Synthetic Peacock dubbing, hare's ear color. **COLLAR:** Arizona Synthetic Peacock dubbing, dark hare's ear color.

Burk's Bottom Roller Hydrop

Hydrop refers to the Hydropsyche caddis, this being an imitation of its larval form.

DRESSING

HOOK: TMC 2457 or similar; sizes 8 to 14. **THREAD:** Olive Ultra Thread, 70-denier. **BEAD:** Black tungsten, 3.3mm for sizes 8 and 10 hooks, 2.8mm for sizes 12 and 14. **WEIGHT:** .020 weighting wire. **RIB:** Fine UFM Superfluoro. **CARAPACE (SHELL):** A strip of Mother of Pearl Sili Skin, tinted with olive over the body and brown at the front with Sharpie markers. **ABDOMEN:** Wapsi Crawdub, pale olive. **COLLAR:** Arizona Synthetic Peacock dubbing, brown.

Burk's Bottom Roller Deep Sherbet

Note: As stated in the preface, substituting materials is a major part of modern fly tying. However, any substitutions in flies like the Burk's Bottom Rollers must be done with great circumspection and attention to maintaining the integrity of the fly's appearance.

DRESSING

HOOK: TMC 2457 or similar; sizes 6 to 10. **THREAD:** Wapsi UTC burnt orange, 70-denier. **BEAD:** Silver tungsten, 3.3mm. **WEIGHT:** .025 weighting wire. **RIB:** 5X monofilament, plain or fluorocarbon. **CARAPACE (SHELL):** A strip of Mother of Pearl Sili Skin, tinted orange with a Sharpie marker. **ABDOMEN:** Rear two-thirds, Wapsi saltwater SLF soft shell #SWD 276; hot spot, Wapsi saltwater SLF fluorescent orange #SWD 503. **COLLAR:** Arizona Synthetic Peacock dubbing, brown

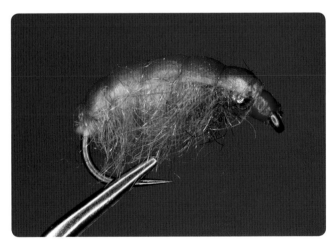

CDC PHEASANT TAIL SOFT-HACKLE
TRAILING SHUCK EMERGER

Ian Cameron is a noted Maine guide who's been kind enough to contribute some of his favorite patterns to this book. In addition to two dry flies, the Melville Bay streamer, and the Red Turck's Tarantula, in this section are three caddis emerger patterns that will catch fish in Maine, and indeed throughout the Northeast and beyond. This is one of them.

> **DRESSING**
>
> **HOOK:** Nymph, wet fly, or dry fly, depending on desired depth; sizes 12 to 18. **THREAD:** To match color of body. **TAIL:** Sparse Antron or Zelon to match color of body. **ABDOMEN:** Pheasant tail, color of choice. **RIB:** Fine copper wire. **THORAX:** Hare's ear or similar; color should be slightly darker than abdomen. **COLLAR:** One CDC feather, color to match body.

> **IAN'S NOTES**
>
> This is an excellent caddis and mayfly emerger pattern. The colors of the components should be matched to prevalent insects. A simple "on the swing" cast with short strips back should produce fish.

COPPER JOHNS

The Fly Shop of Redding, California, has one of the largest and most diversified selections of flies in this business. Tim Fox, the retailing manager, was very helpful in helping me choose flies from their inventory for inclusion in this book. The Copper John, shown here in its basic color and also in red, is one of his contributions. It's become a very popular pattern; I see people fishing it everywhere.

I have included a top-view photo of the basic Copper John so that you tiers can see the details and proportions.

Basic Copper John

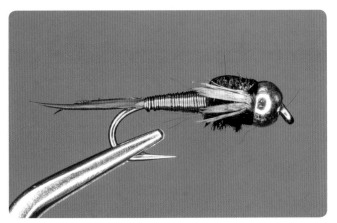

Side view.

Top view.

DRESSING

HOOK: TMC 3761 or similar; sizes 8 to 18 (see tying notes). **THREAD:** Brown or black Danville Flymaster 6/0, Uni-Thread 8/0, or similar. **HEAD:** A gold or copper bead. **TAIL:** Two brown goose biots. **BODY:** Copper Ultra Wire, Uni Soft Wire, or similar; thickness to match hook size. **HIGHLIGHT:** One strand of pearl Flashabou, which will be brought forward over the wing case. **WING CASE:** Dark brown turkey tail or Wapsi Thin Skin. **THORAX:** Peacock herl. **LEGS:** Two small bunches of Hungarian partridge or speckled hen, one on each side.

Red Copper John

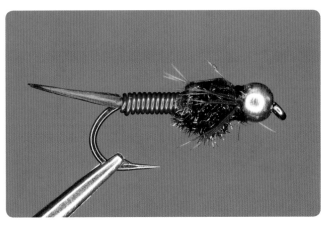

DRESSING

HOOK: TMC 3761 or similar; sizes 8 to 18 (see tying notes). **THREAD:** Black or brown Danville Flymaster 6/0, Uni-Thread 8/0, or similar. **HEAD:** A gold bead. **TAIL:** Two red-dyed goose biots. **BODY:** Red Ultra Wire, Uni Soft Wire, or similar; thickness to match hook size. **HIGHLIGHT:** One strand of pearl Flashabou, which will be brought forward over the wing case. **THORAX:** Peacock herl. **WING CASE:** Dark brown turkey tail or Wapsi Thin Skin. **LEGS:** Two small bunches of Hungarian partridge or speckled hen, one on each side.

TYING NOTES

The components are listed in the order in which they are to be tied on. The TMC 3761 is a 1XL hook, and I find it a bit short for the Copper John. I prefer a 2XL hook, such as the Daiichi 1710.

CZECH NYMPHS

Oliver Nelson, a truly world-class fly tier from England, authored an article in the summer 2006 issue of *Fly Tyer* magazine. Part of it was devoted to Czech Nymphs. He reported that these flies gained international prominence during the Fly Fishing World Championships, where the captain of the Czech team mesmerized Oliver with the incredible effectiveness of the flies and the way in which they were presented. In the article Oliver briefly describes the special method the Czechs used to fish these nymphs, which is a study in and of itself and beyond the purview of a fly-tying book.

Czech Nymph, Olive

There are many variations on the Czech Nymph. To illustrate the tying methodology, here's an olive version.

> **DRESSING**
>
> **HOOK:** Elongated scud; Daiichi swimming larva model 1870 or similar; size 10. **THREAD:** Olive 8/0 Uni-Thread or similar. **SHELL:** A narrow (⅛ inch) strip of a transparent synthetic material. **FIRST RIB (OPTIONAL):** Fine silver oval tinsel. **SECOND RIB:** Very fine monofilament, such as 6X or 7X tippet material. **UNDERBODY:** Weighting wire; here, .015 inch diameter. **BODY:** Sparkly olive dubbing; here, Crawdub from the Spirit River Company. **HOT SPOT (OPTIONAL):** A small ball of bright dubbing or yarn; here, orange. **THORAX:** "Spiky" hare's ear dubbing.

TYING STEPS

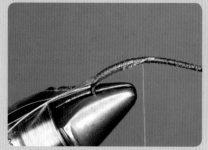

1. Wrap the hook with thread, then tie in the shell material, the tinsel, and the monofilament, in that order.

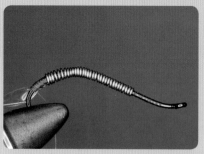

2. Wrap the wire, covering the portion of the hook shown in the photo.

3. Dub the body.

4. Wrap the first rib, counter-wrapping toward yourself.

5. Dub on the hot spot.

6. Dub on the thorax.

CZECH NYMPHS (continued)

7. Finish the fly by bringing the shell material forward over the back of everything, tying it off, and then wrapping the second rib, which is wrapped in the straightforward manner—that is, over and away from yourself.

TYING NOTES

If desired, the shell can be tinted with permanent markers. The first rib can be omitted, at the discretion of the tier. However, the second rib is essential, as it holds everything together. With these slippery synthetic dubbings, the spinning loop method is recommended.

Czech Nymph, Peacock

DRESSING

HOOK: Elongated scud; Daiichi swimming larva model 1870 or similar; size 10. **THREAD:** Purple or black 8/0 Uni-Thread or similar. **SHELL:** A narrow (⅛ inch) strip of a transparent synthetic material. **RIB:** Very fine monofilament, such as 6X or 7X tippet material. **UNDERBODY:** Weighting wire; here, .015 inch diameter. **BODY:** Ice Dub Peacock from Hareline Dubbing. **HOT SPOT (OPTIONAL):** A small ball of bright dubbing or yarn; here, pink. **THORAX:** "Spiky" hare's ear dubbing.

TYING NOTES

Here, the first rib was left off, as I like the material just the way it is.

Czech Nymph, Caddis Green

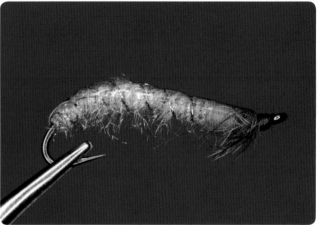

DRESSING

HOOK: Elongated scud; Daiichi swimming larva model 1870 or similar; size 10. **THREAD:** Green or olive 8/0 Uni-Thread or similar. **SHELL:** A narrow (⅛ inch) strip of a transparent synthetic material. **FIRST RIB (OPTIONAL):** Fine gold oval tinsel. **SECOND RIB:** Very fine monofilament, such as 6X or 7X tippet material. **UNDERBODY:** Weighting wire; here, .015 inch diameter. **BODY:** Synthetic dubbing; here, chartreuse Spirit River Brite Blend. **HOT SPOT (OPTIONAL):** A small ball of bright dubbing or yarn; here, hot orange. **THORAX:** "Spiky" hare's ear dubbing.

CZECH NYMPHS (continued)

Czech Nymph, Rust

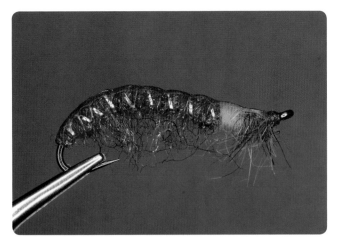

Czech Nymph, Hare-Tron Blend Beadhead

TYING NOTES

Spectrumized blends can be very effective with flies of this type. The dubbing blend starts with gray Hare-Tron from Hareline Dubbing, which is gray rabbit fur and a little Antron, mixed. Small bunches of any soft dubbing in light rust and pale olive are added, then a little fluorescent pink, in this case STS Trilobal Dub, also a Hareline product.

A plain bead will not go around the bend of a hook of this type; thus, the slotted bead. You may have other hooks that won't accommodate a bead. The slotted type will solve that problem. Incidentally, inexpensive hackle pliers with heat-shrink tubing applied to both jaws makes a great bead-grabber.

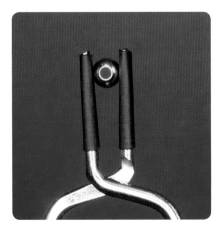

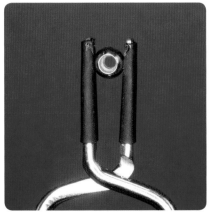

Czech Nymph, Crawdub Blend Beadhead

Czech Nymphs don't lend themselves very well to being tied small. Here's one of mine tied on a smaller hook that works okay, given discretion with the amount and thickness of the dubbing.

DRESSING

HOOK: Scud; Daiichi model 1150 or similar; size 8. **THREAD:** First, red 8/0 Uni-Thread or similar, then finish with gray or black ahead of the bead. **THORAX:** A small silver bead. **SHELL:** A narrow (⅛ inch) strip of a transparent synthetic material. **FIRST RIB:** Silver micro-tinsel or fine wire. **SECOND RIB:** Very fine monofilament, such as 6X or 7X tippet material. **BODY:** A blend; see tying notes. **HOT SPOT:** The bead. **THORAX:** "Spiky" hare's ear dubbing.

TYING NOTES

The dubbing blend combines the following colors of Spirit River's Crawdub: gray, soft shell, and tan, plus a little of Hareline's Ice Dub purple. This being a smaller hook overall, the weighting wire is omitted.

DICK'S BLACK STONEFLY NYMPH

Stoneflies are great trout food. Here's a pattern of mine that I would classify as semi-realistic. It's articulated enough to fool the trout, but not at all tedious and complicated to tie.

DRESSING

HOOK: Curved nymph; here, the Daiichi model 1270; sizes 4 to 14. **THREAD:** Black Uni-Stretch to start with, then black 8/0 Uni-Thread or similar. **UNDERBODY:** Two strips of weighting wire tied along each side of the hook. **BODY:** The black Uni-Stretch. **TAILS:** Black biots. **SHELL/WING CASE:** A strip of black thin Bugskin or Thin Skin (see tying notes); here, the Bugskin. **RIB:** Fine monofilament; plain 3X or 4X leader material will do. **THORAX:** Black Uni-Yarn or dubbing; the Uni-Yarn is used here. **LEGS (HACKLE):** A mottled Brahma hen saddle feather or similar, tied on by the tip end and wrapped and stroked back as a collar.

TYING STEPS

1. Mount the Uni-Stretch in a bobbin and prepare the underbody, per the photo. When the wire strips have been covered entirely, soak the assembly with an adhesive, such as Zap-A-Gap or SureHold. Make sure the glue is completely dry before proceeding.

2. Cut a strip of Bugskin (or Thin Skin) the same width as the underbody assembly and tie it in at the very rear of the hook, pretty-side down, hanging to the rear. Then tie a biot on each side of the rear end of the underbody assembly, and tie in the monofilament ribbing material.

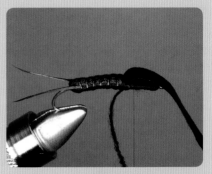

3. Shape the rear part of the body with the Uni-Stretch, then tie it off about midway up the hook or slightly forward of that, and switch to black thread. Fold the Bugskin forward and secure it with the thread, then spiral-wrap the rib and tie off the mono. Fold the Bugskin back out of the way for the moment, and tie in the Uni-Yarn.

4. Form the thorax with the black Uni-Yarn, leaving a little space up front. Tie in the hackle feather by the tip and wrap it in front of the thorax, stroking back the fibers to form a cornucopia.

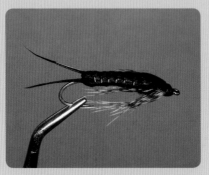

5. Cut off the top fibers of the hackle, then bring the Bugskin forward over the thorax and hackle, trim the excess, and tie off.

TYING NOTES

Bugskin is very finely shaved leather and is available in a wide range of colors and textures. It is sold in fly shops and also at fly-fishing show events in the winter. It makes very attractive wing cases on nymphs. Thin Skin is a product of the Wapsi Company. It is also available in a wide range of colors and some figured patterns as well.

DICK'S PERLA STONEFLY NYMPH

This pattern has been evolving for many years as new materials come along that make it easier to tie—and produce better results. In a variety of sizes and shades, it's proven to be a good imitation of the yellow stoneflies of the Perlidae family, as well as of the large western golden stonefly, *Acroneuria californica*. It's a bit more articulated than my Black Stonefly, in that it features the double wing case and pronotum of the natural insect, but it's still easy to tie.

DRESSING

HOOK: Curved nymph; here, the Daiichi model 1270; sizes 4 to 12. **THREAD:** Bright yellow Uni-Stretch to start with, then brown or camel 8/0 Uni-Thread or similar. **UNDERBODY:** Two strips of thick (.035) weighting wire tied along each side of the hook. **SHELL/WING CASES/PRONOTUM:** Wapsi Thin Skin, labeled Mottled Oak Golden Stone. **TAILS:** Two tan or light brown biots. **RIB:** Fine monofilament. **THORAX SEGMENTS:** Fuzzy dubbing; tan hare's ear works fine. **LEGS:** Three strips of tan speckled Sili Legs, one incorporated in each thoracic segment.

TYING STEPS

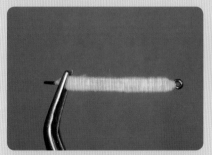

1. Mount the Uni-Stretch in a bobbin and prepare the underbody, per the photo. When the wire strips have been covered entirely, soak the assembly with an adhesive, such as Zap-A-Gap or SureHold. Make sure the glue is completely dry before proceeding.

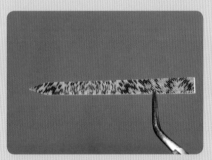

2. Cut a strip of the Thin Skin the same width as the underbody assembly.

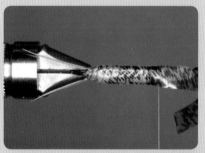

3. Follow the steps for the Black Stonefly until it's time to make the thorax/wing-case assembly. Switch to the thread at this point.

4. Fold back the Thin Skin and tie in the first set of legs with X-wraps. Then dub the first thoracic segment; fold the Thin Skin forward and tie it down, forming the first wing case; and then fold it back again.

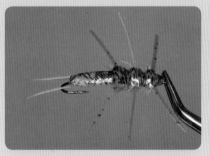

5. Repeat step 4, forming the second wing case and adding the second set of rubber legs. Then fold back the Thin Skin one more time, tie on the third set of legs, and apply a bit more dubbing to form the pronotum. Finish the fly by bringing the Thin Skin forward over the pronotum and tying it off.

If you prefer an alternative to the rubbery leg material, here's a feather-legged version. Everything is the same, except that soft hackle, such as speckled hen or Hungarian partridge, is tied on in two bunches, one under each wing case.

DICK'S ISONYCHIA NYMPH

At one time, five different Isonychias were listed for Eastern trout waters. Thanks to DNA analysis, they were all found to be the same, and are now lumped into the Isonychia bicolor category. Praise the Lord! These slender nymphs are fast swimmers, and the imitations are fished with quick twitches. They move so fast that the trout probably don't get a good look at the white stripe down the back, which is why I list it as optional.

DRESSING

HOOK: Longer nymph; here, the Daiichi model 1750; size 10. **THREAD:** Black or dark brown 8/0 Uni-Thread or similar. **TAILS:** Short, fluffy hen hackle material in mahogany brown. **STRIPE (OPTIONAL):** A piece of thick white thread. **SHELL/WING CASE:** Dark brown Thin Skin or thin Bugskin. **RIB:** Fine monofilament. **BODY/THORAX:** Dark mahogany dubbing. **LEGS:** Short, fluffy hen hackle material in mahogany brown.

TYING NOTES

This fly is tied in the same manner as the Black Stonefly, except that there's no underbody assembly. If you opt for the stripe, tie in the thread after tying the tails and let it hang to the rear. After folding the Thin Skin forward to form the shell, bring the thread over the back, center it, and tie it down. Then wrap the rib and tie off the mono. Fold back the remaining Thin Skin and thread, form the thorax, add the legs, and fold the rest of the Thin Skin forward and tie it off. Then bring the rest of the thread over to the top of the wing case and tie it off, thus completing the fly.

Side view.

Top view.

GUIDE'S SERENDIPITY

This variation of the Serendipity is from Blue Ribbon Flies. Again, the dressing description is theirs, and in this case I suggest using the materials they specify, as the colors and textures have proved to be successful.

DRESSING

HOOK: Tiemco 3761; sizes 14 and 16. **THREAD:** Black and fine; your choice. **BODY:** Dark olive Zelon yarn. **WING:** White Zelon yarn.

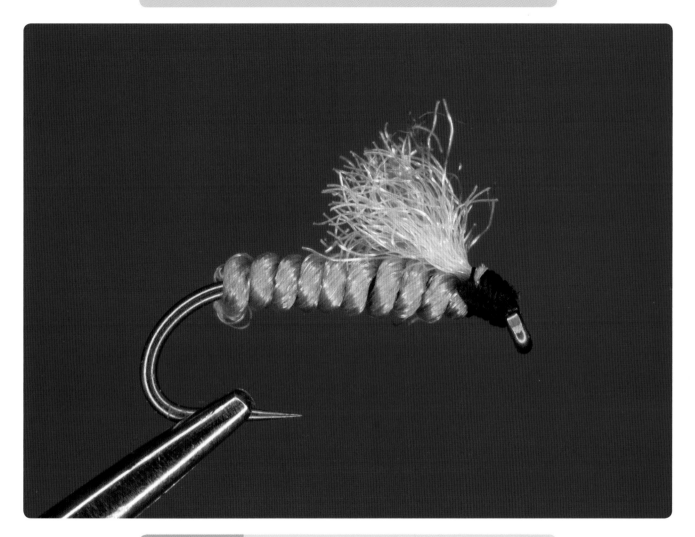

TYING NOTES

Tie on the olive Zelon at the bend. As you wrap forward, twist the strand, thus forming a segmented body. Then tie on the white Zelon, trim it to the length shown, and tie off.

GUMBY LEGS GOLDEN STONEFLY NYMPH

This stunningly realistic imitation of the nymph of the great western golden stonefly, *Acroneuria californica*, is the creation of "Sugar" Keith Tucker. Keith has been fishing and guiding in the Truckee-Tahoe area for ten years, and can be contacted through the Reno Fly Shop.

DRESSING

HOOK: TMC 2457; size 6. **THREAD:** Black 6/0. **UNDERBODY:** V-Rib; two layers on each side of the hook. **SHELL/WING CASES/PRONOTUM:** Wapsi Thin Skin, labeled Golden Stone. **TAILS/ANTENNAE:** Tan or light brown biots. **RIB:** Fine monofilament. **BODY/THORAX:** A blend of Whitlock's Golden Stone SLF and orange Ice Dub. **LEGS:** Gumby legs (see tying notes).

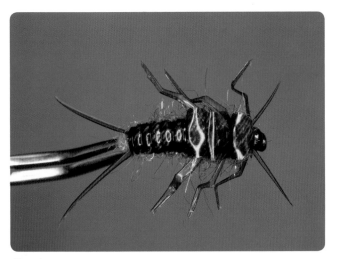

Top view.

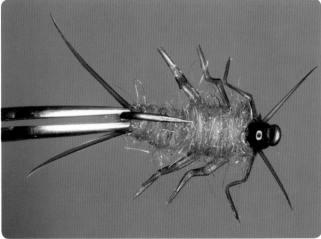

Bottom view.

TYING STEPS

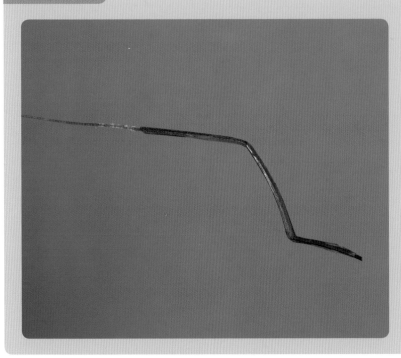

Gumby legs are a Keith Tucker innovation. They are made from goose or turkey biots and very fine, flexible wire. Keith specifies Ultra Wire in brassie size. An adhesive that remains flexible when dry is required; Keith uses Dave's Flexament. Here's the drill:

1. Biots have a convex side and a concave side. Lay them out with the concave sides up.

2. Cut the wire to a length that allows handling: two or three times the length of the biot.

3. Dip one end into the Flexament, and allow the excess to run off.

4. Lay the coated wire into the biots, with the end reaching almost to the tip. If needed, add a little more Flexament with the tip of a toothpick or a bodkin.

5. After the adhesive is completely dry, dip the entire assembly into the Flexament and set aside the biots to dry by sticking the wire into a Styrofoam block. After they have dried, they can be shaped with tweezers.

HOLO SOFTEES

These flies were designed and tied by Bill Ladner, a longtime employee of the Reno Fly Shop. He specializes in catching the giant cutthroats of Nevada's Pyramid Lake, and also spends a lot of time chasing steelhead in the Pacific Northwest. He uses the Holo Softee and the Holomidge throughout the West with great success.

This pattern may also be tied in black, green, and gold by using those colors of holographic tinsel for the bodies.

Red Holo Softee

Plum Holo Softee

DRESSING

HOOK: TMC 2487; sizes 12 to 18. **THREAD:** Black 6/0 or 8/0. **BODY:** Red holographic tinsel. **RIB:** Fine chartreuse Ultrawire. **THORAX:** Peacock herl. **WING CASE:** Rad floss, pearl. **HACKLE:** Speckled brown hen neck feather.

DRESSING

HOOK: TMC 2487; sizes 12 to 18. **THREAD:** Black 6/0 or 8/0. **BODY:** Plum holographic tinsel. **RIB:** Fine chartreuse Ultrawire. **THORAX:** Peacock herl. **WING CASE:** Rad floss, pearl. **HACKLE:** Speckled brown hen neck feather.

HOLOMIDGES

These flies were also designed and tied by Bill Ladner. The pattern may also be tied in black, gold, and purple by using those colors of holographic tinsel for the bodies.

Red Holomidge

DRESSING

HOOK: TMC 2487; sizes 14 to 18. **THREAD:** Black 6/0 or 8/0. **BODY:** Red holographic tinsel. **RIB:** Fine chartreuse Ultrawire. **THORAX:** Peacock herl. **WING BUDS:** Red holographic tinsel.

Green Holomidge

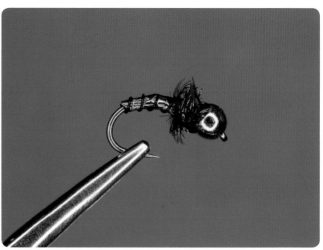

DRESSING

HOOK: TMC 2487; sizes 14 to 18. **THREAD:** Black 6/0 or 8/0. **BODY:** Green holographic tinsel. **RIB:** Fine chartreuse Ultrawire. **THORAX:** Peacock herl. **WING BUDS:** Green holographic tinsel.

THE JAILBIRD

This simple yet remarkably effective pattern is the brainchild of lady-guide Marla Blair and is copyrighted in her name. Marla guides in Massachusetts and Connecticut, and is noted for her expertise on the Farmington River. The Jailbird works best tied small; I carry it in sizes 14 down to 20. It is fished with weight added to the leader and usually with a strike indicator.

Those of us who have fished with Marla have used the Jailbird on various rivers and have found it to be pretty much universally effective. It has taken Great Lakes steelhead on New York's Salmon River and large rainbow trout in the Rockies.

DRESSING

HOOK: Shrimp/scud; here, the Daiichi model 1150; sizes 12 to 18. **THREAD:** Red; Marla uses 6/0 or 8/0 Uni-Thread, depending on hook size. **WING CASE (FOR LACK OF A BETTER NAME):** A strip of white closed-cell foam, doubled. **BODY:** Olive-colored dubbing.

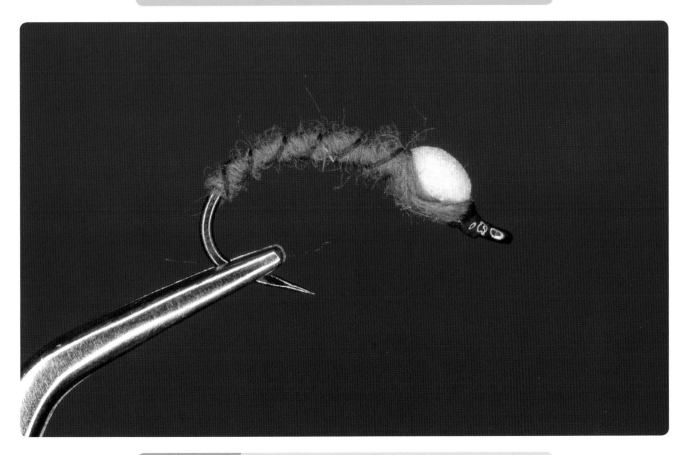

TYING NOTES

Tie in the foam strip on the "crown" of the hook, fold it forward and tie it down just short of the eye, then fold it rearward over itself, tie it down, and trim off the excess. Apply the dubbing and X-wrap it in front of the foam bump, crossing over underneath it. Wrap the dubbing well down around the hook bend, and after it's been expended, wrap forward, using the thread as ribbing. Try to estimate the amount of dubbing required to cover to the midpoint of the bend.

The tying sequence for the Jailbird is shown in considerable detail in a recent book of mine, *Inside Fly Tying*. If further instructions are required, that's where you'll find them.

MAGIC EMERGER

This pattern was contributed by Ian Cameron.

DRESSING

HOOK: Curved caddis; sizes 12 to 18. **THREAD:** Brown, tan, or olive. **TAIL:** Wood duck flank. **ABDOMEN:** Brown, tan, or olive SLS (Synthetic Living Fiber), loop dubbed, sparse. **RIB:** Fine copper wire. **WING:** Mylar sheathing, cut tent-style with the points toward the tail. **ANTENNAE:** Wood duck flank; one fiber on either side pointed back toward the hook bend. **HEAD:** Loop dubbed SLS of the same color as the abdomen, slightly larger in diameter than the abdomen.

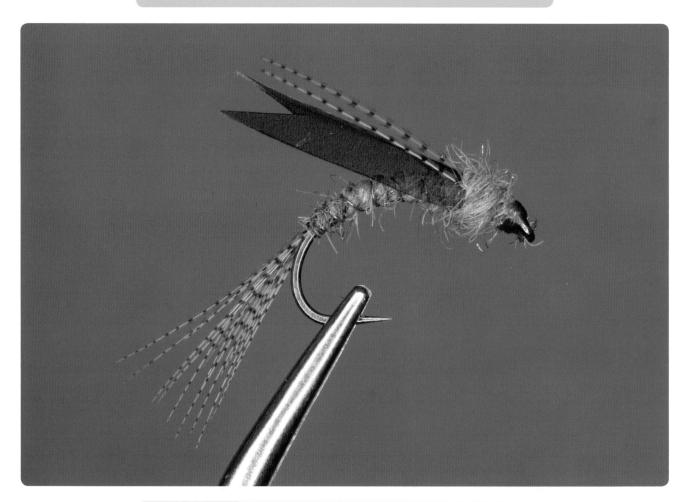

IAN'S NOTES

The wing on this "magic" fly is Shane Stalcup's Mylar sheathing, but a piece cut from a plastic bag works well enough. Adding a bead of gold, copper, or glass will get the fly down a little farther in the water column. This fly works year-round on the rivers I guide on, especially in October on the East Outlet of the Kennebec.

AUTHOR'S NOTES

A scud hook also works fine. In tying this fly, I used Wapsi's Thin Skin as a substitute for the Mylar sheathing, and Spirit River's Crawdub as a substitute for the SLF. The reason is that they are very close in appearance and texture, and were in my inventory.

MARCH BROWN HEN WING EMERGER

This is another pattern from *Hatch Guide for New England Streams*, by Thomas Ames. The insect imitated is *Stenonema vicarium*, the American march brown. Tied with a light hen feather, it also imitates the former gray fox, *Stenonema fuscum*, now also *S. vicarium*. As of this writing, I've not yet had a chance to fish this fly, but my Catskill spies report that it's a killer.

DRESSING

HOOK: Typical dry fly; Daiichi model 1180 or similar; sizes 8 and 10. **THREAD:** Rust or camel 8/0 Uni-Thread or similar. **TAIL:** Three pheasant tail fibers. **BODY:** Pale cream dubbing (see tying notes). **HACKLE:** Speckled hen saddle feather, just two turns. **WING:** The tip end of the hackle feather, tied back flat over the body.

TYING STEPS

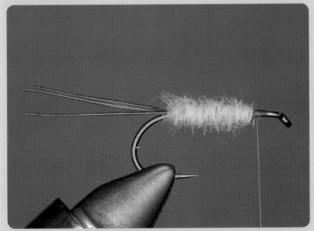

1. Tie on the tails and dub the body.

2. Wrap a turn or two of the hen feather as hackle and finish with it extending out to the front.

TYING NOTES

The dubbing in the Ames book is simply blended Australian possum. I wasn't sure exactly what that meant, so for color I'm going by the photo in the book, and also by my own observations.

3. Bring the feather back into the position shown in the photo and secure it there with thread wraps.

MARCH BROWN NYMPH

The march brown (*Stenonema vicarium*) nymph is rather distinctive. It's a flat-bodied clinger type, with powerful legs and long tails. The underside is a shade of pale orange or amber, the exact color depending on the streambed coloration. I don't bother to tie strips of weighting wire along the sides of the hook to make this nymph more flat, as I do with my stoneflies, because this is ungainly on a smaller hook, and the trout don't seem to care.

This pattern also covers the former gray fox (*Stenonema vicarium*), which is no longer so classified. It is now lumped with the march brown, as DNA has proven that they are one and the same bug. Color and size variations caused the earlier confusion. This is one of my favorite nymphs, as the *S. vicarium* populations are still quite good in the streams of the Northeast that I love to fish.

This nymph is similar in construction to many others, in that the shell and wing case material is tied in upside-down and hanging to the rear, to be folded forward after the other components have been tied in place.

DRESSING

HOOK: 1XL nymph; here, the Daiichi model 1560; sizes 8 to 12. **THREAD:** Camel or brown 8/0 Uni-Thread or similar. **UNDERBODY:** Built up and tapered with brown Uni-Stretch. **TAIL/BODY:** A bunch of long fibers from a cock ringneck pheasant tail. **SHELL/WING CASE:** Mottled brown, thin Bugskin. **RIB:** Fine monofilament. **BELLY:** Amber dubbing. **LEGS:** A brownish speckled Hungarian partridge feather; either a small bunch of barbs tied on at the throat or the feather itself, tied in by the tip and wrapped as a soft hackle.

MICRO MADISON BEADHEAD

More from Blue Ribbon Flies. This fly was originated by guide Geoff Unger to imitate a number of small mayfly nymphs that populate the Madison River in Montana, which it does very effectively.

DRESSING

HOOK: Dai-Riki 075; size 18. **THREAD/BODY:** Tan 8/0 Uni-Thread. **HEAD:** 1.5mm copper bead. **TAIL:** Hungarian partridge dyed brown. **RIB:** Small brown UTC wire. **THORAX:** Brachycentrus olive Zelon dubbing. **WING CASE:** Medium-width pearlescent Mylar.

TYING NOTES

The thread forms the body. After wrapping the rib, tie in the Mylar and let it hang to the rear. Dub the thorax, bring the Mylar over the top of it, and tie off. *Brachycentrus*, by the way, is a prominent genus within the caddis family, Brachycentridae.

THE MONTANA

This is a very good general stonefly nymph pattern, and is easy enough to tie that even the virtual beginner can do it. It's commonly tied in either black or brown, with either a yellow or orange chenille thorax. I caught a lot of trout on the Montana back in the 1960s and '70s, before siltation completely ruined my much-loved Esopus Creek. It was a classic stonefly stream.

Black Montana

DRESSING

HOOK: Long nymph, 3XL or 4XL; here, the Daiichi model 1270; sizes 6 to 12. **THREAD:** Black 8/0 Uni-Thread or similar. **TAIL:** A short bunch of webby black hackle. **UNDERBODY (OPTIONAL, BUT RECOMMENDED):** Weighting wire, .015 inch diameter. **BODY/WING CASE:** Fine to medium black chenille. **THORAX:** Fine to medium yellow or orange chenille. **LEGS:** Two or three turns of webby black hackle.

TYING STEPS

1. Tie on the tail and wrap the wire forward into the thorax area. Then wrap the chenille body, covering about two-thirds of the hook shank. At that point, form a loop with the chenille, tie it down, and fold it back. You now have three strands of chenille with which to form the wing case.

2. Tie in the hackle, then tie in the yellow chenille, wrap the thorax, and tie off and trim the chenille. Take two, or at the most three, turns of hackle, spiral-wrapping it through the yellow chenille, and trim off those on top. Finish the fly by bringing the three strands of black chenille forward over the yellow and tying off the material.

Brown Montana

See tying steps under Black Montana.

DRESSING

HOOK: Streamer, 6XL; the Daiichi model 2220 or similar; sizes 6 to 12. **THREAD:** Brown 8/0 Uni-Thread or similar. **TAIL:** A short bunch of brown hackle. **UNDERBODY (OPTIONAL, BUT RECOMMENDED):** Weighting wire, .015 inch diameter. **BODY/WING CASE:** Fine to medium brown chenille. **THORAX:** Fine to medium yellow or orange chenille. **LEGS:** Two or three turns of brown hackle.

THE PARA-DORITO

My friend and colleague Marla Blair came up with this emerger pattern. It got its name from an incident on the Farmington River, where Marla guides. Her client was taking a lunch break, snacking on Doritos, and Marla was giving the new fly a workout. The trout were gobbling it. The client observed that the trout seemed to be eating the fly as fast as she was eating the Doritos. Thus, the Para-Dorito!

DRESSING

HOOK: Light-wire scud; here, the Daiichi model 1130; sizes 12 to 18. **THREAD:** Red 6/0 or 8/0 Uni-Thread or similar. **WING POST:** A pearl synthetic yarn, such as Hi-Vis, Antron, Zelon, etc., or white CDC. **TAIL:** Synthetic yarn, same as the wing post. **BODY:** Marla's dubbing mix: olive, mahogany, golden tan, cream. **HACKLE:** Ginger, barred ginger, straw cream, or medium gray dun.

THE PEA-CABOU

This is another very simple pattern that will take trout most anywhere. The name is derived from the two materials it employs: peacock and marabou. A friend and I were fishing a lake in Montana, using imitative Callibaetis nymphs, but we ran out. I tied on a brown Pea-Cabou. Our guide scoffed, but the fly soon made a believer out of him. That evening he tied three dozen of them.

DRESSING

(BROWN, OLIVE, OR BLACK)

HOOK: 1XL or 2XL nymph; here, the 1XL Daiichi model 1560; sizes 8 to 12. **THREAD:** Brown, camel, olive, or black 8/0 Uni-Thread or similar. **HACKLE:** A bunch of brown, olive, or black marabou fibers, tied in at the front and facing forward. **TAIL:** Another bunch of marabou fibers; brown, olive, or black. **BODY:** A bunch of peacock herl fronds.

TYING STEPS

1. Tie in the hackle bunch first, just short of the eye, with the tip ends sticking out frontward.

2. Tie in the tail in the rear. As for the peacock, I prefer to tie in the bunch by the tip end and twist it together with one strand of 8/0 Uni-Thread, thus forming a virtual chenille. After tying off the peacock up front, stroke back the hackle fibers and wrap in front of them, thus forming a collar.

Olive Pea-Cabou.

Black Pea-Cabou.

PHEASANT TAIL BEAD THORAX (PTBT) NYMPHS

I started tying this style of nymph shortly after beads designed for fly tying came onto the market. The positioning of the bead creates a realistic-looking wing case, and also adds weight to the fly. Brass beads are shown here. If more weight is wanted, tungsten beads can be used. Tungsten beads are much heavier than copper ones, by a ratio of 2.6 to 1, according to my powder scale. That's very significant.

Except on large nymphs, a single bundle of pheasant tail fibers—say, eight to ten—will suffice for both tail and body. On larger nymphs, or if you don't have a tail with very long fibers, tie the tail and then use another bunch for the body.

Begin by de-barbing the hook and sliding the bead into place. Beads made for fly tying have a larger hole on one side than the other. Insert the hook point into the smaller hole, so that the larger one faces rearward. Given a modicum of neatness when wrapping the tying thread, this enables the bead to cover all or most of the thread used to tie in the wing case material. After tying in said material, tie off, then tie on again in front of the bead. This positions the thread for locking the bead in place and finishing the fly. The two dressings—plain and olive—are tied in the same manner. An English hackle plier with shrink-wrap tubing added to both jaws makes an excellent bead gripper.

Pheasant Tail Bead Thorax (PTBT) Nymph

DRESSING

HOOK: Basic 1XL or 2XL nymph; here, the 1XL Daiichi model 1560; sizes 10 to 18. **THREAD:** Brown or camel 8/0 Uni-Thread or similar. **THORAX:** A copper bead; sized in proportion to the hook. **UNDERBODY (OPTIONAL):** Brown Uni-Stretch. **TAILS/BODY:** Cock ringneck tail fibers. **RIB:** Fine copper wire. **WING CASE:** Dark brown or gray Thin Skin. **LEGS:** Pheasant tail fibers or dark brown soft hackle barbs around the bottom and sides.

TYING STEPS

1. Tie a short tail, then fold back the remainder of the pheasant tail fibers for use as the body. Tie in the ribbing wire.

2. Unless a very slender silhouette is wanted, build an underbody with the Uni-Stretch. Then wrap the pheasant fibers forward to the thorax area, and reverse-wrap the rib.

3. Tie on the Thin Skin over the front of the body material and let it hang to the rear. Move the bead into place, allowing it to cover the thread wraps as much as possible.

4. Finish the fly by adding the legs, then bringing the Thin Skin forward over the bead to the front and tying it off.

Olive Pheasant Tail Bead Thorax (PTBT) Nymph

DRESSING

HOOK: Basic 1XL or 2XL nymph; here, the 1XL Daiichi model 1560; sizes 10 to 18. **THREAD:** Camel or olive 8/0 Uni-Thread or similar. **THORAX:** A gold bead; sized in proportion to the hook. **UNDERBODY (OPTIONAL):** Olive Uni-Stretch. **TAILS/BODY:** Pheasant tail fibers or soft hackle barbs, dyed olive. **RIB:** Fine gold wire. **WING CASE:** Dark olive, brown, or gray Thin Skin. **LEGS:** A small bundle of olive-dyed pheasant tail fibers, deployed around the bottom and sides.

TYING NOTES

Feel free to use on these nymphs whatever you have for legs that closely resembles what is listed. This would include hen hackle, soft rooster hackle, Hungarian partridge, whatever. Remember the Cow Credo: If it eats grass, gives milk, and goes "moo," it's a cow.

POOPAHS

Tim Fox of The Fly Shop of Redding has graciously sent me two of his original dressings. He calls them Poopahs. There are more Poopahs in the series, and they can be seen by going to The Fly Shop's Web site (www.flyshop.com; click on the catalog, then go to the flies section). These are very fishy-looking flies, and Tim reports having fished them with telling effect.

Fox's GB (Gold Bead) Poopah, Olive

Side view.

Top view.

DRESSING

HOOK: TMC 3769 or similar; size 12. **BEAD:** Gold bead, 7/64 inch size. **THREAD:** Black Danville Flymaster 6/0 or similar. **BODY:** Olive Vernille, aka Ultra Chenille, fine or regular size. **UNDERBODY:** Medium pearl tinsel. **RIB:** Gold brassie-size Ultra Wire or similar. **LEGS:** Hungarian partridge or mottled hen saddle. **ANTENNAE:** Two wood duck flank fibers, one on each side of the fly. **COLLAR:** Black ostrich herl.

Fox's CB (Copper Bead) Poopah, Cinnamon

DRESSING

HOOK: TMC 3769 or similar; size 12. **BEAD:** Copper bead, 7/64 inch size. **THREAD:** Tobacco brown Danville Flymaster 6/0 or similar. **BODY:** Cinnamon (Poopah brown) Vernille, aka Ultra Chenille, fine or regular size. **UNDERBODY:** Medium pearl tinsel. **RIB:** Gold brassie-size Ultra Wire or similar. **LEGS:** Hungarian partridge or mottled hen saddle. **ANTENNAE:** Two wood duck flank fibers, one on each side of the fly. **COLLAR:** Brown ostrich herl.

PRINCE NYMPH, BEADHEAD

This is another of those flies that no one can say specifically what it imitates, but we love it, and so do the fish. It bears the name of its originator, Doug Prince. The beadhead is a recent addition, and a most effective one. There are several accepted dressings, but this one is my favorite. And by the way, if anyone knows the derivation of the term *biot*, I'd love to hear it.

DRESSING

HOOK: Nymph; here, the 1XL Daiichi model 1560; sizes 10 to 14. **THREAD:** Black 8/0 Uni-Thread or similar. **HEAD:** A gold bead. **TAIL:** Two brown biots. **RIB:** Narrow oval gold tinsel. **BODY:** Peacock herl. **HACKLE:** Brown. **WINGS:** Two white biots.

TYING NOTES

I like to reverse-wrap the ribbing tinsel. That way, it doesn't simply fall into the ridges of the peacock herl, and it also adds durability.

ANTRON PRINCE NYMPH

This is another of Buddy Knight's patterns, and he tied the fly in the photograph. It's a very interesting variation of the Prince Nymph, one that I can't wait to try on my home waters in North Carolina.

TYING STEPS, PER BUDDY

1. Slide on the bead and mount the hook in the vise.
2. Wrap on ten turns of the weighting wire and push it forward against the rear of the bead.
3. Tie in a 2-inch piece of red Antron that is half the thickness desired for the tail. Tie it in by the middle at the center of the hook, to the rear of the wire. Wrap to the rear, covering the yarn, then double it back and wrap forward.
4. Tie in the ribbing tinsel.
5. Tie in four peacock herls, wrap them forward, and tie them off. Then wrap the rib.
6. Tie in a piece of the white wing material twice as long as the finished wing will be, and half the thickness. Tie it in behind the bead by the middle, then double it back to form the wing.
7. Strip off the barbs from one side of the hen hackle, tie it in by the tip, and wrap only one turn. This finishes the fly.

TELLICO NYMPH

This pretty pattern was sent to me by Jeff Curtis of Curtis Wright Outfitters, located in Weaverville, North Carolina. I had asked Jeff to suggest a few patterns that were popular on the streams of the Great Smokies. He chose the Tellico nymph and three drys that may be seen in the Dry Flies chapter, because they are effective on the wild-trout and delayed-harvest waters in his area.

DRESSING

HOOK: Nymph; here, the 2XL Daiichi model 1710; sizes 10 to 14. **THREAD:** First, bright yellow Uni-Stretch bobbin-mounted, then black 8/0 Uni-Thread or similar. **TAIL:** Strands of golden pheasant tippet. **SHELL:** A narrow strip from a brown turkey feather, prepared as per the tying notes. **RIB:** A single narrow peacock herl, preferably taken from the longer-fronded side of a peacock sword feather. **UNDERBODY (OPTIONAL):** Fine weighting wire. **BODY:** The bright yellow Uni-Stretch, or bright yellow floss, if you prefer. **HACKLE:** Brown.

TYING STEPS

1. The bright yellow Uni-Stretch is mounted in a bobbin. The beginning of the body is shown here.

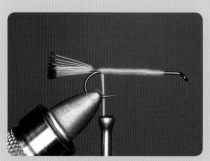

2. Tie on and attach the tail.

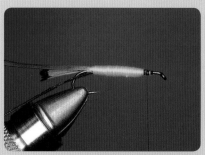

3. Tie in the turkey strip upside-down and hanging to the rear. Then tie in the peacock herl, finish shaping the body with the Uni-Stretch, then switch to the regular black tying thread.

4. Spiral-wrap the peacock herl, then wrap a short collar, using a soft hackle.

5. Stroke the hackle barbs down on each side and finish the fly by bringing the turkey strip over the back and tying it off at the front.

TYING NOTES

Prepare the turkey strip ahead of time by saturating it with a flexible adhesive and allowing it to dry. Note that the components are listed in the order in which they are attached. Tie on the tail, then tie in the shell strip, followed by the peacock herl. If you've opted for weighting wire, cut short the butt ends of the components you've tied in thus far and abut them with the weighting wire.

THE $3 (THREE DOLLAR) DIP

This is one of six very interesting patterns contributed by Blue Ribbon Flies, a truly excellent shop and outfitting service located in West Yellowstone, Montana. BRF is run by fly fishers for fly fishers. A number of great patterns have originated there, including the simple yet deadly Sparkle Dun with the shuck-dragger tail that accounts for a multitude of trout out West every season.

From whence the odd name? There's a bridge on the Madison River where the landowner allows anglers to park for $3 a day. The fly is a variation of the Seren*dip*ity; thus, the $3 Dip.

> **DRESSING**
>
> This is the dressing exactly as specified by BRF. Feel free to make substitutions for such components as the hook, thread, and rib, provided they are very close to the originals.
> **HOOK:** Shrimp/scud; Dai-Riki 135; sizes 14 to 18. **HEAD:** A small gold bead. **BODY/THREAD:** Danville Flymaster 6/0 in olive, brown, or red, or pearl Krystal Flash. **RIB:** Small gold UTC wire.
> **WING:** A small clump of deer hair, trimmed short.

WEST BRANCH CADDIS EMERGER

This is another pattern contributed by Ian Cameron.

DRESSING

HOOK: Dry fly; sizes 12 to 18. **THREAD:** To match color of body. **BODY:** Sparse gray, olive, or tan dubbing. **WING:** One white-tipped breast feather from a male wood duck or mallard, tied tent-style and curving downward. **HACKLE:** Brown to light brown, one turn.

West Branch Caddis Emerger, a tying step.

West Branch Caddis Emerger, bottom view.

West Branch Caddis Emerger.

West Branch Caddis Emerger, tied as a dry fly with different hackle.

IAN'S NOTES

Credit for this fly goes to Eddie Reif of Eddie's Flies and Tackle, Bangor, Maine. Ed was a mentor of mine, and I learned a lot from him before his untimely passing. This is actually one hot fly for the West Branch of the Penobscot, where I guide a lot. Possible variations include a trailing shuck as well as a thorax of peacock herl. If you add several turns of hackle to the head, it's a great dry fly for caddis.

WHITLOCK'S GBRL (GOLD BEAD RUBBER LEG) RED FOX SQUIRREL NYMPH

As is the case with a number of the flies in this book, this unique pattern came to me from The Fly Shop of Redding. It's an original from Dave Whitlock, who has long been known for his innovative designs. I have listed the dressing as it was given to me by Tim Fox of The Fly Shop, and it is suggested that any substitutions be made with strict attention to the coloration and texture of the fly. The body and thorax materials are specific Dave Whitlock blends, and I would recommend no substitutions be made. Ditto with the Sili Legs material.

> **DRESSING**
>
> **HOOK:** TMC 5262 or similar; sizes 6 to 14. **THREAD:** Danville Flymaster 6/0 coffee (#429). **HEAD:** A gold bead. **TAIL:** A small, short bunch of red fox squirrel tail hair. **BODY:** Whitlock's SLF blend dubbing, red fox squirrel nymph abdomen. **RIB:** Gold wire. **THORAX:** Whitlock's SLF blend dubbing, red fox squirrel nymph thorax. **COLLAR:** Natural brown schlappen. **LEGS:** Two strands of Sili Legs pumpkin/black flake, one on each side just behind the bead.

Side view.

Bottom view.

ZUG BUG

The Zug Bug is a time-proven general nymph pattern. I like peacock-bodied flies any time I'm fishing where there are rainbow trout, as they seem to like eating peacock herl.

DRESSING

HOOK: 1XL or 2XL nymph; here, the 2XL Daiichi model 1710; sizes 10 to 16. **THREAD:** Black 8/0 Uni-Thread or similar. **TAIL:** A small bunch of peacock sword fibers. **RIB:** Narrow oval silver tinsel. **BODY:** Peacock herl. **HACKLE:** Brown. **WING CASE:** A trimmed-to-shape mallard flank feather, dyed wood duck color.

6

General Streamers

AWESOME LAKE BROOKIE

This is a pattern I put together during my week at Awesome Lake, Labrador, in the summer of 2003. I noticed that whenever a small brook trout was hooked, large ones came out of nowhere and tried to eat it. So I accommodated them with this pattern, and it worked.

DRESSING

HOOK: Typical long streamer; 7XL Daiichi model 2370 or similar; size 2 and longer. **THREAD:** Start with orange (pumpkin) Uni-Stretch, then switch to olive 8/0 Uni-Thread or similar. **TAIL:** Olive marabou. **RIB:** Narrow red Mylar tinsel, well-spaced. **BODY:** The pumpkin Uni-Stretch. **BELLY:** White bucktail tied beneath the hook. **THROAT:** Bright orange hackle barbs. **WING:** Olive marabou. **TOPPING:** A few strands of peacock herl over the top of the wing. **HEAD/EYES:** Stick-on or painted-on eyes, coated with a strong adhesive.

TYING NOTES

After wrapping the body with the Uni-Stretch, switch to the olive thread.

BLACK-NOSED DACE, A NEW VERSION

This traditional Catskill streamer first appeared, to my knowledge, in 1947 in Art Flick's *Streamside Guide to Naturals and Their Imitations*. It is included here because it still works. In fact, it works quite well, even where the natural baitfish doesn't exist. On the advice of master guide George Kelley, I fished it on the Bighorn River, and it was amazingly effective. I've redesigned it a bit.

DRESSING

HOOK: Typical streamer; here, the 7XL Daiichi model 2370; sizes 2 to 8. **THREAD:** Black Uni-Stretch, mounted in a bobbin. **TAG:** A very short bunch of red yarn. **BODY:** Pearlescent or silver braid. **BELLY:** White hair—bucktail or whatever—tied beneath the hook. **WING, LAYER 1:** Black hair, to represent the stripe that runs the length of the body on the natural. **WING, LAYER 2:** Light brown hair, to represent the back of the natural. **HEAD/EYES:** Stick-on or painted-on eyes, coated with a strong adhesive.

TYING NOTES

The hair used for this fly should be fine and straight. The brown hair for the back can be found on some, but not all, bucktails. Using Uni-Stretch for the tying thread automatically builds up the head to accept the eyes. I recommend that before the stick-on eyes are pressed on, or the painted eyes dotted on, a coat of clear head lacquer be applied and allowed to dry completely. Then flatten the head a little with flat-jawed pliers.

Inexpensive water-based art paints make great eyes. They can be dotted on using the rear ends of drill bits. For the protective layer, epoxy is the toughest. Another that I like a lot is Soft Body from Angler's Choice. It's a water-based adhesive, and you'll want the thicker of the two viscosities. Try to use it up fairly soon, as the shelf life is limited.

CLOUSERS

The Clouser Minnow, as it is known generically, is one of the most important developments in modern fly tying and fishing. The addition of weight near the front end of the fly, in the form of bead chain eyes or dumbbells, has two significant effects: It causes the hook to ride point-upward, and it gives the fly a jigging action. The design has been widely copied, but so far as I know, Bob Clouser was the originator and deserves the credit.

Rainbow Clouser

The pattern shown here is an imitation of a baby rainbow trout. Much as we like to ennoble our favorite fish, they do eat their young, given the opportunity.

> **DRESSING**
>
> **HOOK:** Saltwater hook with a chrome finish; here, the 3XL Daiichi model X472; sizes 2 to 8. **THREAD:** White Uni-Stretch or similar. **EYES:** Chrome bead chain. **BELLY:** White synthetic hair (craft fur). **BODY LAYERS:** Synthetic hair (craft fur), in this order: soft pink, topped by greenish olive, topped by medium gray. **ADHESIVE:** A superglue, such as Zap-A-Gap or SureHold.

TYING STEPS

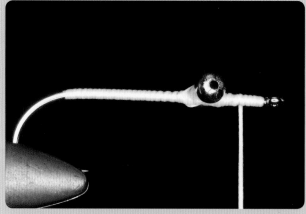

1. With the hook in the normal position, wrap a layer of the Uni-Stretch at the front and X-wrap the bead chain in place. After the first few X-wraps, add a drop of superglue and continue. Then cover the hook with Uni-Stretch.

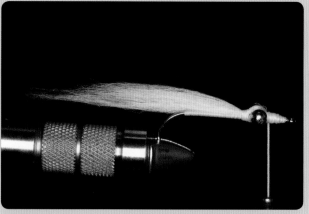

2. Tie on the white hair in front of the eyes, then pass it between them and secure it with a few thread wraps to the rear of the eyes.

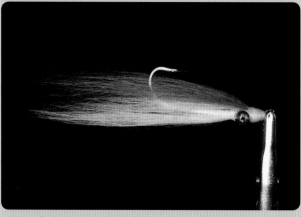

3. Turn the hook over and add the three layers of body hair.

TYING NOTES

I like Uni-Stretch for tying on dumbbells and bead chains, because it has enough body to make a good foundation and enough strength to enable very tight wraps, and it absorbs adhesives very well. On smaller Clousers, I may switch to regular thread after tying on the dumbbell and the belly hair, so as to avoid creating too much bulk when adding the rest of the materials.

I should mention that the Spirit River Company is an excellent source for the various dumbbells used for the Clousers and for the stranded flashy material used for the highlights. They offer a type of dumbbell that has receptacles for stick-on eyes, and you can buy them as sets, so that a perfect fit is guaranteed. I have found that if the fit is proper, the eyes stay attached indefinitely.

Catfish Clouser

This Clouser pattern is an imitation of a baby catfish, or bullhead. It's a useful pattern in many of our bass fisheries and also in tailrace trout fisheries.

DRESSING

HOOK: Long nymph or streamer; sizes 2 to 6. **THREAD:** Start with white Uni-Stretch or similar; finish with black Uni-Stretch or similar. **EYES:** Gold dumbbell with receptacles for stick-on inserts. **BELLY:** White synthetic hair (craft fur). **HIGHLIGHT:** A pearl flashy material; here, Spirit River Spectra Splash. **BACK:** Black or very dark brown synthetic hair (craft fur). **ADHESIVE:** A superglue, such as Zap-A-Gap or SureHold.

Mickey Finn Clouser

This Clouser is simply the old Mickey Finn streamer, tied with synthetic materials. It's still a very useful pattern when a brightly colored streamer is wanted.

DRESSING

HOOK: Long nymph or streamer; sizes 2 to 10. **THREAD:** Start with bright yellow Uni-Stretch or similar; finish with black thread. **EYES:** Eyed silver dumbbell shown here, or one with receptacles for stick-on inserts. **BODY:** Silver tinsel or braid. **BELLY:** Yellow synthetic hair (craft fur). **MIDDLE LAYER:** Red synthetic hair (craft fur). **BACK:** Yellow synthetic hair (craft fur), approximately equal to the two lower layers combined. **ADHESIVE:** A superglue, such as Zap-A-Gap or SureHold.

Sculpin Clouser

This pattern is so-named for two reasons: It rides hook-upward, so that it can be fished along the streambed with minimal snagging, and the mottled hair of the fox squirrel tail suggests the markings of a sculpin.

DRESSING

HOOK: Wet fly or nymph; here, the Daiichi model 1550; sizes 4 to 8. **THREAD:** Start with any color of Uni-Stretch; finish with tan thread. **EYES:** Gold dumbbell. **BELLY:** Beige or light tan synthetic hair (craft fur). **HIGHLIGHT:** A gold flashy material; here, Spirit River Spectra Splash. **BACK:** Hair from the bottom side of a fox squirrel tail. **ADHESIVE:** A superglue, such as Zap-A-Gap or SureHold.

HEN HACKLE STREAMERS

A few years ago, Dr. Tom Whiting sent me some hen pelts and asked me what applications they might have in fly tying. They included various bloodlines and breeds, and both capes and saddles. As it turned out, they produced, among other things, great streamers, which was not something one would expect. The cape feathers have the ideal shape for making baitfish imitations, and the web in the center has just the right amount of opaqueness. When combined with some flashy body material and a wisp of hair for the belly, some wonderful effects result.

The trick is to envelop the body, rather than position the feathers atop the hook. I see that the immortal Carrie Stevens tied many of her flies in that manner. My favorite streamer hook is the Daiichi model 2370, which I designed. I incorporated a looped eye to facilitate piling materials onto the front of the hook. However, for this style of streamer, it's a little easier to get the feather to lie flat along the sides when a regular eyed hook is used.

For larger flies, the Mike Martinek Rangeley Streamer hook is a good choice. These are available in many fly shops or on the Web at www.belvoirdale.com. The Daiichi models 2461 and 2462, which come in black and chrome finishes, respectively, also work well.

The Winnie Boy

A prime example of this type of streamer is the Winnie Boy. This is a design of mine for imitating the smelt of New Hampshire's Lake Winnipesaukee. It works well wherever freshwater smelt are found.

DRESSING

HOOK: Long streamer, as referred to above; sizes 2 to 8. **THREAD:** Gray or black 8/0 Uni-Thread or similar. **UNDERBODY:** Pearl or rainbow flat braid. **BELLY:** White bucktail. **WINGS (BODY):** Pale gray hen feathers (see tying notes). **CHEEKS:** Hen saddle feathers, either plain gray or with barring. **EYES:** Stick-ons.

TYING NOTES

It's necessary to make an assembly consisting of the eyes, cheeks, and a body feather. Stick the eyes in place on the cheeks, then lay the cheeks on a piece of waxed paper, eye-side down. Place a small droplet of Elmer's Glue or something similar on the back of the eye, which can be seen through the cheek feather. Then lay the two body feathers, a front and a back, over the cheeks in the position they will be in when the fly is assembled. Allow the glue to dry before finishing the fly.

I started out using Zap-A-Gap for making these assemblies, but that stuff is hard to control and is very unforgiving if a mistake is made. Elmer's is much easier to control, and it dries clear.

Usually, I use only one feather on each side, as the hen feathers have a lot of density in the center, and I want the sparkle of the underbody to glow through. However, most traditional streamers call for two feathers front and back, spooned. If you opt for using the feathers in pairs, you can either include the inner feathers in the assembly process, or simply add them when tying the wings onto the hook.

Tie on the wings one at a time, front assembly first. Tilt them slightly inward, so that the front and back feathers come together on top. It's easier to get the assemblies to lie in place if you catch a bit of the delta of the front, rather than just the quills.

The Winnie Boy body and belly.

The completed Winnie Boy fly.

The Dr. Tom

This is a typical hen streamer pattern. I named it for Dr. Tom Whiting, without whose magnificent hen feathers these flies wouldn't exist. I'm using a hen cape that has a distinct bronzish tint, but that's not essential. This fly is much smaller than the Winnie Boy, so the cheeks can be omitted as they are here, in which case the eyes are stuck directly onto the main feathers and fixed in place with the glue.

> **DRESSING**
>
> **HOOK:** Long streamer, same as for the Winnie Boy; sizes 2 to 8. **THREAD:** Gray, black, or brown 8/0 Uni-Thread or similar, depending on the color of the feathers. **UNDERBODY:** Gold or silver flat braid. **BELLY:** White bucktail. **WINGS (BODY):** Gray hen feathers; the exact shade may vary. **CHEEKS (OPTIONAL):** Hen saddle feathers, either plain gray or with barring. **EYES:** Stick-ons.

THE HORNBERG, ALSO CALLED THE HORNBERG SPECIAL

In the form in which it's now generally tied throughout the Northeast and beyond, the Hornberg must be classified as a streamer. It got its start in Wisconsin, and was tied by Frank Hornberg, the originator, as a dry fly. Somehow it got altered in its migration eastward.

DRESSING

HOOK: Long streamer 3XL to 6XL; here, the 4XL Daiichi model 1750; sizes 2 to 8. **THREAD:** Black 8/0 Uni-Thread or similar. **UNDERBODY:** Silver flat tinsel or braid. **UNDERWING:** Yellow; could be hen hackle tippets or a bunch of soft hair. **WINGS (BODY):** Two barred mallard flank feathers, with the cupped sides facing inward. **EYES:** Jungle cock or a substitute (see tying notes). **HACKLE:** Grizzly.

TYING STEPS

1. Wrap a double layer of silver tinsel or braid, covering about three-fourths of the hook shank. Then tie in a bunch of yellow hair.

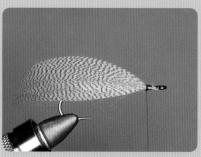

2. Tie on the front and rear wing feathers, one at a time.

3. If you're rich, go for real jungle cock here. If not, select a dotted guinea fowl feather that has a white dot centered on the quill near the tip.

4. Trim the feather to shape and tie it in place as you would jungle cock.

5. Adding a grizzly hackle completes the fly.

TYING NOTES

Real jungle cock is in short supply and is quite expensive. After the import ban in the late 1960s, tiers—myself included—started to simply omit this component. The flies didn't fish worth a damn; hence, substitutions. Here, I've taken a dotted guinea fowl feather and trimmed it so that only a single dot, centered on the quill, is left. I wouldn't use this on a classic salmon fly, but for a "meat" fly like the Hornberg, it does the job.

INSTANT SUSHI BAITFISH

This fly is the design of Mike Martinek and is the result of his experiments with an interesting synthetic hair product he calls Electric Sushi. When used in the conventional manner, it tends to be rather brittle. This is counteracted, however, by tying it on in small clumps at three to five spots along the hook. The clumps are then picked out with a bodkin. The final shaping of the fly is obtained by simply pinching off small bunches of material with one's fingers. The result is a durable, lifelike, three-dimensional baitfish imitation that is very light and doesn't retain water during false casting.

Electric Sushi is available from Mike, whose phone number is (781) 944-8744. It comes in a number of colors, but Mike says his preference for this fly is blue and opal pearl mixed together. (*Note:* Electric Sushi is similar to a synthetic called Angel Hair from a company named Angler's Choice, also known as Gone Fishin' Enterprises, Inc.)

Final enhancements include adding a gill slash, using a red Sharpie marker, and gluing on synthetic eyes, either flat or 3-D.

DRESSING

HOOK: Typical saltwater, 2/0 to 2. **THREAD:** White Danville Flat-Waxed Nylon. **BODY:** As described above, Electric Sushi in blue and opal pearl mixed; tied on in small clumps, working along the hook from rear to front. **GILLS:** Applied with a red Sharpie marker. **EYES:** Stick-on, either flat or 3-D.

LEW OATMAN'S STREAMERS

By the time this book is published, Lew Oatman will have been gone for fifty years, but his beautiful and productive flies maintain his legacy. He was a Battenkill fisherman and tied to imitate the baitfish found there. Other than that, there's little known about the man. I wasn't able to find out much on the Web, other than that he died in 1958 and that his flies are very collectible.

So Lew was four years dead before I first fished the Battenkill, but his flies were de rigueur, especially his original streamer designs. It's been a while since my Battenkill days, but my friends back home still fish the river, and they tell me that Lew's flies still work. And I can promise you that they'll take fish in many other streams as well.

Golden Darter

DRESSING

HOOK: Typical long streamer; 7XL Daiichi model 2370 or similar; sizes 4 to 10. **THREAD:** Black 8/0 Uni-Thread or similar. **TAIL:** Two small sections from left and right silver pheasant wing feathers. **RIB:** Narrow to medium silver tinsel, depending on hook size. **BODY:** Yellow floss or Uni-Stretch. **THROAT:** The tips of two small saddle feathers from the rear of a jungle cock cape. **WING:** Two or four golden badger hackles, depending on hook size. **EYES:** Here, real jungle cock.

Silver Darter

DRESSING

HOOK: Typical long streamer; 7XL Daiichi model 2370 or similar; sizes 4 to 10. **THREAD:** Black 8/0 Uni-Thread or similar. **TAIL:** Two small sections from left and right silver pheasant wing feathers. **RIB:** Narrow to medium flat silver tinsel, depending on hook size. **BODY:** White floss or Uni-Stretch. **THROAT:** A few fronds from a peacock sword feather. **WING:** Two or four silver badger hackles, depending on hook size. **EYES:** Jungle cock.

TYING NOTES

In Lew's day, jungle cock was plentiful and inexpensive. I realize that's no longer the case, but in recognition of Lew's artistry, I have used it on his patterns herein. For flies to take fishing, feel free to use the guinea fowl substitute shown with the Hornberg, or else build up the head and use painted or stick-on eyes. In addition, acceptable substitutes for the little jungle cock saddle tips that are used for the Golden Darter's throat can be found on several lines of hen saddles, notably the Brahma.

Shushan Postmaster

DRESSING

HOOK: Typical long streamer; 7XL Daiichi model 2370 or similar; sizes 4 to 10. **THREAD:** Black 8/0 Uni-Thread or similar. **TAIL:** Two small sections from left and right mottled turkey quills. **RIB:** Narrow to medium flat gold tinsel, depending on hook size. **BODY:** Light yellow floss or Uni-Stretch. **THROAT:** Opposing sections from left and right red-dyed duck or goose feathers. **WING:** Hair from a fox squirrel tail. **EYES:** Jungle cock (see Golden Darter tying notes).

MATUKAS

The Matuka style of streamer offers an alternative design. One of its main attributes is that it has less of a tendency to tangle around the bend of the hook during casting, because the "wing," if I might call it that, is secured along the length of the hook shank.

Perhaps the most popular material used for tying the Matuka is rabbit, meaning strips cut from a tanned hide. These are readily available in many natural and dyed colors. A couple of years ago, while attending the Fly Tackle Retailer's Show in Denver, I noticed a display of rabbit pelts that had interesting barred dye jobs. They were laid out in quite an array, and looked like they all had colorful pajamas on. The exhibitor was Rob McLean, who does business as Freestone Flies & Guide Service out of Saratoga, Wyoming. He generously gave me some samples, and you're about to see the results here.

The key to easy Matuka tying is multi-bobbin operation. Materials suspended by the weight of the bobbin leave the hands free to operate on the delicate ribbing process that is the essence of Matuka tying. Note that on any of these flies you can substitute other hooks. I don't want to send you scavenging for hooks you probably don't have.

Green-Barred Rabbit Matuka

DRESSING

HOOK: Short streamer; 4XL Daiichi model 1750 or similar; sizes 4 to 8. **THREAD:** Start with white Uni-Stretch, then switch to white Uni-Cord (see tying steps). **UNDERBODY (OPTIONAL):** .015-inch-thick weighting wire, fed out of a bobbin. **RIB:** Narrow gold oval tinsel, also fed out of a bobbin. **BODY:** The white Uni-Stretch. **WING:** A rabbit strip. **HEAD:** Green deer hair spun and trimmed Muddler-style **EYES (OPTIONAL):** Holographic 3-D eyes, set in Goop.

TYING STEPS

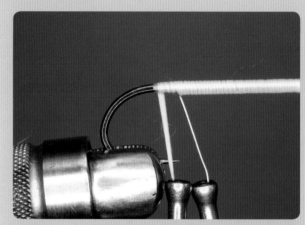

1. Wrap a couple of layers of white Uni-Stretch, then tie in the wire, working toward the hook bend. End up with the Uni-Stretch a few turns to the rear of the wire.

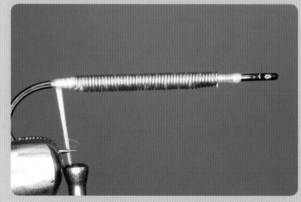

2. Wrap the wire forward, ending well short of the hook eye.

MATUKAS (continued)

3. Cover the wire with the Uni-Stretch, and in the process tie in the tinsel at the bend of the hook. Note that the tinsel is also mounted in a bobbin. Then wrap forward to the front of the hook.

4. Tie on the rabbit strip, then tie off the Uni-Stretch, so that there is no bobbin at the front to bother the ribbing process.

5. Separate the fur, exposing the hide, and make two tight wraps of tinsel at the bend of the hook. Pull on the rabbit strip from the rear so that it's tight along the top of the hook. Then start working forward, repeating the first step of the ribbing but taking only one turn of tinsel at each pass. A toothpick is a handy tool when executing the ribbing.

6. Complete the ribbing, tie on with the Uni-Cord, and use it to tie off the tinsel, concurrently making a smooth base for spinning the hair. Then spin on and trim the deer hair. If you haven't opted for eyes, the fly is done.

7. The fly with eyes added.

Tan-Barred Rabbit Matuka

DRESSING

HOOK: Short streamer; 4XL Daiichi model 1750 or similar; sizes 4 and 6. **THREAD:** Start with white Uni-Stretch, then switch to brown 8/0 Uni-Thread or similar. **RIB:** Narrow gold oval tinsel, fed out of a bobbin. **BODY:** The white Uni-Stretch. **WING:** A rabbit strip. **COLLAR:** Mottled hen hackle, one or two feathers wrapped collar-style.

Chartreuse Rabbit Matuka

DRESSING

HOOK: Chromed, 3X or 4X long; Daiichi model X474 or similar; sizes 2/0 to 4. **THREAD:** Start with white Uni-Stretch, then switch to green or chartreuse 8/0 Uni-Thread or similar. **RIB:** Fine monofilament, fed out of a bobbin. **BODY:** The white Uni-Stretch. **WING:** A rabbit strip. **BELLY (OPTIONAL):** White hair, natural or synthetic. **COLLAR:** Rabbit fur, same as the wing, tied as a collar.

Purple-Black-Barred Rabbit Matuka (Alaska Fly)

DRESSING

HOOK: Salmon; Daiichi model 2421 or similar; sizes 2 to 6. **THREAD:** Black 8/0 Uni-Thread or similar. **RIB:** Fine monofilament, fed out of a bobbin. **BODY:** Silver braid. **WING:** A rabbit strip. **COLLAR:** Rabbit fur, same as the wing, tied as a collar. **NOTE:** The hook listed above does not come in a size larger than a 2. If you want to tie the fly larger, feel free to substitute whatever hook you feel will work.

Red-Yellow-Barred Rabbit Matuka (Pike Fly)

DRESSING

HOOK: Saltwater; Daiichi model X452 or similar; sizes 2/0 to 2. **THREAD:** Start with bright yellow Uni-Stretch, then switch to red 8/0 Uni-Thread or similar. **RIB:** Silver wire, fed out of a bobbin. **BODY:** The bright yellow Uni-Stretch. **WING:** A rabbit strip. **COLLAR:** Red and yellow hackle, the two feathers wrapped together collar-style.

MATUKAS (continued)

Hen Matukas

Matukas are also tied using feathers. Hen saddles make great Matukas and are easy to work with. Because of their webbiness, two feathers, rather than four, make really nice flies. Some hen capes are also good for Matuka tying, provided they have sufficient body and a baitfish-like shape. These pelts are available in a wide range of natural and dyed colors and are inexpensive. The tying techniques are the same as rabbit Matukas.

Speckled Hen Matuka

DRESSING

HOOK: Short streamer; 4XL Daiichi model 2461 or similar; sizes 2 to 8. **THREAD:** Start with white Uni-Stretch, then switch to 8/0 Uni-Thread or similar. **RIB:** Fine monofilament, fed out of a bobbin. **BODY:** The white Uni-Stretch. **WING:** Two speckled hen cape or saddle feathers, with the dull sides facing inward. Remove some of the bottom fibers, so that the feathers fit over the body, as shown. **COLLAR:** A soft hen hackle tied as a collar; color to match or complement the wing.

Rainbow-Barred Hen Matuka

DRESSING

HOOK: Short streamer; 4XL Daiichi model 2461 or similar; sizes 2 to 8. **THREAD:** Black 8/0 Uni-Thread or similar. **RIB:** Fine monofilament, fed out of a bobbin. **BODY:** Rainbow braid material. **WING:** Two pale grizzly hen cape or saddle feathers, with the dull sides facing inward. Remove some of the bottom fibers, so that the feathers fit over the body, as shown. **COLLAR:** A soft hen hackle tied as a collar; color to match or complement the wing.

MATUKABOUS

The Matukabou is Mike Martinek's variation of the standard Matuka, which uses wire, tinsel, monofilament, or something else to secure the wing. Instead, Mike ties the body in stages and adds a wing segment with each body segment. The flies shown here were tied by Mike.

Yellow Matukabou

DRESSING

HOOK: Typical stout streamer; Daiichi model 2220 or similar; sizes 2 to 8. **THREAD:** 6/0 Danville Flymaster, 8/0 Uni-Thread, or similar. **TAIL:** Yellow marabou. **BODY:** Yellow chenille, tied in four sections. **WING:** Yellow marabou, tied in four sections, coinciding with the body. **THROAT:** Red soft hackle. **EYES:** Stick-on type.

White Matukabou

DRESSING

HOOK: Typical stout streamer; Daiichi model 2220 or similar; sizes 2 to 6. **THREAD:** 6/0 Danville Flymaster, 8/0 Uni-Thread, or similar. **TAIL:** White marabou. **BODY:** White sparkle chenille, tied in four sections. **WING:** White marabou, tied in four sections, coinciding with the body. **THROAT:** Red soft hackle. **EYES:** Stick-on type.

Green Matukabou

DRESSING

HOOK: Typical stout streamer; Daiichi model 2220 or similar; sizes 2 to 6. **THREAD:** 6/0 Danville Flymaster, 8/0 Uni-Thread, or similar. **TAIL:** Green marabou. **BODY:** Green cactus chenille, tied in four sections. **WING:** Green marabou, tied in four sections, coinciding with the body. **THROAT:** Red soft hackle. **EYES:** Stick-on type.

MUDDLER MINNOWS

This is one of those older flies that are still very effective. The original dressing predates World War II. The design is credited to Don Gapen and was intended to imitate the sculpins that were native to the Lake Nipigon watershed, which is located within the province of Ontario, north of Lake Superior. Since then, many variations have appeared. The Basic Muddler Minnow below is what I understand to be the original dressing, except that I've substituted gold braid for flat gold tinsel. I don't know if the original was tied weighted, as I've tied it here.

Mottled turkey wing feathers were practically a giveaway when Mr. Gapen tied the first Muddler. Since that breed of turkey is no longer the one sold for food, the feathers are now rather pricey. As of this writing (September, 2007) a prime pair is selling for $6 to $7. It is, therefore, advisable to fully utilize them.

Formerly, the Muddler wings and tails were formed in the same manner as traditional wet-fly wings. Two opposing feathers were required, a left and a right. A small section was cut from the leading edge of each feather, and the pair was then seated atop the hook and tied on. The trailing sides of the feathers were simply discarded.

I'd like to offer this alternative: Cut a section from the trailing edge of a single feather that is twice as wide as you'll need. Fold it double, and trim it to shape. A pair of curved scissors is helpful here. The Basic Muddler in the photos was tied using this technique. Note the shapely, well-marked wing and tail.

Basic Muddler Minnow

DRESSING

HOOK: Mid-length streamer, 4XL to 6XL; here, the 4XL Daiichi model 1750; sizes 4 to 12. **THREAD:** First, camel or brown 8/0 Uni-Thread or similar; then a specialized thread for the deer-hair work, such as Uni-Nylon 210-denier or a gel-spun thread, such as Uni-Cord 100-denier (see thread notes). **TAIL:** Two sections of mottled turkey tail, tied in the same manner as a standard wet-fly wing. **WEIGHT:** Formerly, lead wire; now, lead wire substitute. **BODY:** Gold braid. **UNDERWING:** A small bundle of gray squirrel tail hair. **WING:** Two sections of mottled turkey tail. **HEAD/COLLAR:** Soft, "pulpy" deer body hair (see hair notes).

THREAD NOTES

The so-called gel-spun threads and the Uni-Nylon threads share some characteristics. They both tend to lie flat—which is great when that suits the task at hand. However, this needs to be controlled, because if the thread spreads floss-like and individual fibers are exposed, they will break and a hairball will result. If you see this about to happen, spin the bobbin a few times to bring the thread fibers back together.

When tying on and spinning/stacking hair, spin the bobbin so the thread becomes narrow, rather than flat. I refer to this as "sharpening" the thread.

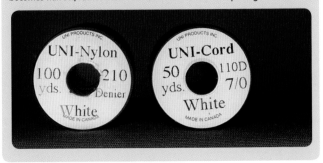

HAIR NOTES

For success in making Muddler-type head/collars, it's essential to have the right hair for the job, meaning the right texture and the right length. The term *pulpy* means that the hair is very soft and will readily flare and spin under thread tension. As for length, the head/collar assembly on a typical Muddler should be equal to about the front third of the overall length of the fly or perhaps slightly less than that. Keep this in mind when buying hair, and think about what size Muddlers you'll be tying.

As to the amount of hair, the hair-spinning gurus use the term *pencil*: One pencil is equal to the thickness of a common wooden pencil. For the average-size Muddler, one generous pencil is sufficient to form the head and collar. On larger Muddlers, or where a larger head is desired, more hair can be used initially, or the first bunch can be supplemented with an additional bunch, taken from the butt part.

MUDDLER MINNOWS (continued)

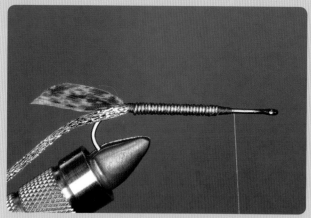

1. After tying the tail, tying in the braid, and wrapping the weighting wire, it is advisable to apply a thin coating of superglue along the top of the wire, so that it seeps into the wraps and bonds the assembly.

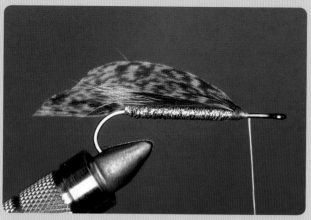

2. Tie on the squirrel tail underwing, keeping it sparse. Then tie on the main wing. At this point, tie off the thread and tie on the specialized thread that will be used to configure the head/collar. Here, Uni-Cord 100-denier is being used.

3. Cut off a bundle of deer hair, comb out any underfur and short stuff, and use a hair evener (also called a stacker) to even up the tips. You may want to trim the butts a little, as this makes them easier to deal with after the hair has been spun on. Hold the bundle against the top of the hook, allowing it to shroud down around the sides a little. Now take three wraps of thread precisely on top of one another under gradually increasing tension, and apply maximum tension with the final wrap. If you're stacking, hold the hair in position. If you're spinning, release it. In either case, follow up with several very firm wraps, each on top of the other. Then slide the thread forward through the butts, stroke them into an upright position, and make some wraps tight to the front. Having thus secured the hair, tie off.

TYING NOTES

Spinning vs. stacking: With spinning, the hair bundle is released when maximum thread pressure is applied, and it will deploy itself around the hook. With stacking, the tier continues to hold on to the hair as maximum thread pressure is applied, and it will deploy itself around approximately the top and sides of the hook. Thus, if you like your Muddler heads and collars to be flat on the bottom, stacking will work best.

Finishing notes: I recommend using a few extra turns when whip-finishing with gel or nylon threads. I also suggest the use of superglue as head cement, as these threads are awfully slippery and finish knots can come undone.

Trimming notes: Hopefully you have scissors that have small serrations on one blade, as these will grip the hairs effectively. A curved-bladed scissor makes shaping the head easier. It is advisable, at least in the beginning, to trim with the scissor tips pointing rearward. Trimming with the tips pointing forward causes the hairs to be raised unevenly as the scissor blades close, and the result is a raggedy-looking head. Trim off all of the butt ends and then work back into the collar hairs slightly, as this forms a smooth transition.

The great masters of hair-tying often use razor blades instead of scissors. The best razor blades are the old double-sided type, but they are very hard to come by and also potentially dangerous. I use a razor blade to flatten the bottom of a hair bunch, when that's the effect I want. They can be purchased in quantity in hardware stores. You'll find that they have a short life, as cutting hair quickly dulls them.

Kennebago Muddler

Side view.

Bottom view.

DRESSING

HOOK: Typical streamer; here, the 7XL Daiichi model 2370; sizes 4 to 12. **THREAD:** First, camel or brown 8/0 Uni-Thread or similar; then a specialized thread for the deer-hair work, such as Uni-Nylon 210-denier or a gel-spun thread, such as Uni-Cord 100-denier. See thread notes for the Basic Muddler. **WEIGHT (OPTIONAL):** Formerly, lead wire; now, lead wire substitute. **BODY:** Silver flat tinsel (unweighted) or silver braid (weighted). **UNDERWING:** A small bundle of gray squirrel tail hair. **WING:** A large, center-quilled mallard or teal flank feather. **HEAD/ COLLAR:** Soft, "pulpy" deer body hair. See Basic Muddler hair notes.

TYING NOTES

The very front of the winging feather is wrapped with thread, so that it envelops the body, as the photos show. At this point, tie off the regular thread and tie on the specialized thread that will be used to configure the head/collar. Here, Uni-Nylon 210-denier is being used. Finish the fly in Muddler fashion.

White Marabou Muddler

DRESSING

HOOK: Typical streamer; here, the 7XL Daiichi model 2370; sizes 2 to 10. **THREAD:** White Uni-Nylon 210-denier or a gel-spun thread, such as Uni-Cord 110-denier. See Basic Muddler thread notes. **TAIL:** White marabou. **WEIGHT (OPTIONAL):** Formerly, lead wire; now, lead wire substitute. **BODY:** Pearlescent or silver braid. **WING:** White marabou. **HIGHLIGHT (OPTIONAL):** A few strands of flashy stuff, such as Krystal Flash, along the sides of the wing. **HEAD/COLLAR:** Soft, "pulpy" white deer body hair. See Basic Muddler hair notes.

TYING NOTES

Because marabou is so pliant and easy to work with, it's okay to use the spinning thread throughout. The marabou tail contributes to the overall silhouette, so that the wing can be tied short enough to minimize tangling around the hook.

MUDDLER MINNOWS (continued)

Black Marabou Conehead Muddler

DRESSING

HOOK: Typical streamer; here, the 6XL Daiichi model 2220 (see tying notes); sizes 2 to 10.
THREAD: First, black 8/0 Uni-Thread or similar; then black Uni-Nylon 210-denier or a gel-spun thread, such as Uni-Cord 110-denier, black. See Basic Muddler thread notes. **HEAD:** A black cone head; tungsten is recommended. **TAIL:** A short piece of red yarn. **BODY:** Pearlescent braid. **WING:** Black marabou. **HEAD/COLLAR:** Soft, "pulpy" black deer body hair. See Basic Muddler hair notes.

TYING NOTES

A cone head can be incorporated in practically any Muddler-type fly, including the original. However, the hook must have a round or approximately round bend to accommodate the typical cone. Hooks with more compound bends, such as sproat and Limerick hooks, can accept slotted cones, which are available these days.

A cone is an effective embellishment, and you'll be surprised at how easily it fits in with the head/collar. When tying off, simply slide the thread against the rear of the cone head. When trimming, the head actually becomes a continuation of the cone's shape.

THE SAVAGE SEDUCER

This fly takes its name from one of my favorite fishing partners, Sim Savage. We were fishing in high-water conditions one spring, and Sim showed me a bushy streamer fly that he thought might work. It was tied completely out of grizzly hackles. I was experimenting with some Coq de Leon hen feathers, and decided to substitute them for the grizzly. We've been catching fish with the fly ever since. The cone or beadhead is listed as optional, but it enhances the fly so much that I no longer tie the Savage Seducer without one or the other.

Detailed tying steps for this fly appear in my book *Inside Fly Tying*, under the name Sim's Seducer. I've decided I like Savage better, so I've renamed it.

DRESSING

HOOK: Short to mid-length streamer; here, the 4XL Daiichi model 1750; sizes 4 to 8. **THREAD:** Black or dark brown 8/0 Uni-Thread or similar. **HEAD (OPTIONAL):** A cone or beadhead. **TAIL:** Two or four (depending on hook size) Coq de Leon hen feathers, with the cupped sides facing inward. **BODY:** Coq de Leon hen feathers folded and tied in by the tips, then wrapped forward; as many as required to complete the fly.

TYING STEPS

1. Slide the cone or bead onto the hook. If using a bead, insert the hook point into the smaller side of the hole. Tie on the tail feathers—either one on each side or a pair on each side—at the rear of the hook.

2. Prepare the body feathers by folding them as you would when tying a collar hackle. Tie on the first one where the tail joins the hook and wrap it forward, stroking back the barbs.

3. Tie off the first feather and wrap additional feathers until the fly is completed.

THE BRAHMA SUTRA

This fly is quite similar to the Savage Seducer but uses different feathers. Chicabou, a registered trade name of Whiting Farms, is used for the tail. It is found at the posterior of certain hen saddle pelts—in this case, a hen of the Brahma breed.

DRESSING

HOOK: Long nymph to short streamer; here, the 4XL Daiichi model 1750; sizes 4 to 8. **THREAD:** 8/0 Uni-Thread or similar; color to match the fly. **HEAD (OPTIONAL):** A cone or beadhead. **TAIL:** A Chickabou feather, as described above. **BODY:** Brahma hen saddle feathers, folded and tied in by the tips, then wrapped forward; as many as required to complete the fly.

TYING STEPS

1. Chicabou comes from the butt end of Brahma hen pelts, as well as certain other breeds. It is tied on Woolly Bugger–style for the tail, as the finished fly photo shows.

2. Brahma hen saddle feathers like this one take the place of the Coq de Leon feathers used for the Savage Seducer and are wrapped in exactly the same manner.

3. The finished fly. Note the tungsten beadhead.

SOFT-HACKLE STREAMERS FROM GARTSIDE

Jack Gartside is an excellent fly designer. Some of his flies look improbable, to say the least, but they work very well indeed. More details can be found on his Web site, www.jackgartside.com, along with other interesting and entertaining information.

The Soft-Hackle Streamer can be tied in plain colors, such as the basic white one shown in the tying steps, and in a number of color combinations, two of which are included here. The original version had no bead or cone head, because those items didn't yet exist. I list them as optional, but I highly recommend them.

Gartside's Soft-Hackle Streamer, White

DRESSING

HOOK: Mid-length (2XL or 3XL) wet fly; here, the 3XL Daiichi model 1720; sizes 2 to 8. **THREAD:** Black 8/0 Uni-Thread or similar. **HEAD (OPTIONAL):** A cone or beadhead. **HIGHLIGHT:** One or two strands of silver Flashabou, tied in near the middle of the hook and doubled rearward. **MAIN HACKLE:** One large white marabou feather. **FRONT HACKLE:** One or two mallard or teal flank feathers, wrapped as a collar.

TYING STEPS

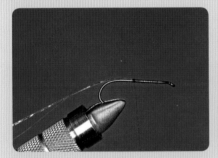

1. Tie in the Flashabou and double it rearward, as shown.

2. Tie in the marabou feather by the tip end and wrap it forward, stroking back the fronds with each wrap, making sure they all encircle the hook (see tying notes).

3. Do likewise with the front hackle feather.

Gartside's Soft-Hackle Streamer, Olive-Yellow

DRESSING

HOOK: Mid-length (2XL or 3XL) wet fly; here, the 3XL Daiichi model 1750; sizes 2 to 8. **THREAD:** Camel, brown, or black 8/0 Uni-Thread or similar. **HEAD (OPTIONAL):** A gold beadhead. **HIGHLIGHT:** One or two strands of gold Flashabou, tied in near the middle of the hook and doubled rearward. **MAIN HACKLE:** One yellow and one bright olive marabou feather. **FRONT HACKLE:** One or two yellow-dyed mallard or teal flank feathers, wrapped as a collar.

Gartside's Soft-Hackle Streamer, Black-Olive

DRESSING

HOOK: Mid-length (2XL or 3XL) wet fly; here, the 3XL Daiichi model 1750; sizes 2 to 8. **THREAD:** Black 8/0 Uni-Thread or similar. **HEAD (OPTIONAL):** A black or nickel silver cone head. **HIGHLIGHT:** One or two strands of gold Flashabou, tied in near the middle of the hook and doubled rearward. **MAIN HACKLE:** One black and one olive marabou feather. **FRONT HACKLE:** A black webby hackle feather, such as schlappen, wrapped as a collar.

TYING NOTES

On the Olive-Yellow streamer, the yellow feather was tied in first and wrapped halfway to the bead, then the olive feather was tied in and wrapped forward, leaving only enough space for the front hackle. With the Black-Olive streamer, the two marabou feathers were tied in together and wrapped as one. It's your choice.

STANLEY STREAMERS

Dave Stanley has been the proprietor of the Reno Fly Shop and Truckee River Outfitters for the past twenty-five years. He's one of the most highly regarded anglers and fly shop owners in the country. When not managing the two shops, guiding, or traveling to fish, Dave is usually pursuing his other great passion, duck hunting in the Great Basin.

Stanley Streamer Little Brown Trout

Stanley Streamer Little Rainbow Trout

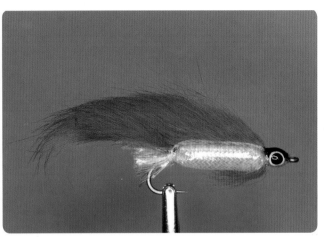

DRESSING

HOOK: TMC 9395; size 6. **THREAD:** Danville Flat Waxed Nylon, yellow. **WEIGHT:** 0.25 weighting wire. **UNDERBODY:** Yellow chenille. **BODY:** Pearl Mylar tubing. **GILLS (THROAT):** A tuft of orange rabbit fur. **WING:** Dark brown rabbit strip. **HEAD/EYES:** Painted (see tying notes).

TYING NOTES

The dorsal surface of the head is painted on with acrylic paint, as are the eyes. The head and body are finished with a thin coat of Five-Minute Epoxy. The wing strip is glued in place along the top of the body, also with Five-Minute Epoxy. These notes apply to all of the Stanley Streamers.

DRESSING

HOOK: TMC 9395; size 6. **THREAD:** Danville Flat Waxed Nylon, pink. **WEIGHT:** 0.25 weighting wire. **UNDERBODY:** White chenille. **BODY:** Pearl Mylar tubing. **GILLS (THROAT):** A tuft of red rabbit fur. **WING:** Olive rabbit strip. **HEAD/EYES:** Painted. See tying notes for the Stanley Streamer Little Brown Trout.

Stanley Streamer Dace

DRESSING

HOOK: TMC 9395; size 6. **THREAD:** Danville Flat Waxed Nylon, red. **WEIGHT:** 0.25 weighting wire. **UNDERBODY:** Red chenille. **BODY:** Pearl Mylar tubing. (**NOTE:** The body is tied with pearl Mylar tubing, just like the others. The red chenille underbody makes it look orange.) **GILLS (THROAT):** A tuft of orange rabbit fur. **WING:** Dark brown rabbit strip. **HEAD/EYES:** Painted. See tying notes for the Stanley Streamer Little Brown Trout.

NOTE: The body of the Dace pattern is tied with pearl Mylar tubing, just like the others. The red chenille underbody makes it look orange.

Stanley Streamer Sunfish

DRESSING

HOOK: TMC 9395; size 6. **THREAD:** Danville Flat Waxed Nylon, chartreuse. **WEIGHT:** 0.25 weighting wire. **UNDERBODY:** Chartreuse chenille. **BODY:** Pearl Mylar tubing. **GILLS (THROAT):** A tuft of orange rabbit fur. **WING:** Olive rabbit strip. **HEAD/EYES:** Painted. See tying notes for the Stanley Streamer Little Brown Trout.

WOOLLY BUGGERS

I have included only three Woolly Buggers in this book, because I believe everyone is quite familiar with both the patterns and the tying steps. Also, a very comprehensive and detailed book dedicated to Bugger-ology is already available. It's titled *Woolly Wisdom*, by Gary Soucie, and is published by Frank Amato Publications.

Woolly Bugger, Black-Grizzly-Peacock

This is one of my favorite Woolly Buggers, here tied with a cone head.

DRESSING

HOOK: Mid-length streamer; here, the 4XL Daiichi model 1750; sizes 4 to 8. **THREAD:** Black 6/0 or 8/0 Uni-Thread or similar. **HEAD:** A cone, black nickel or chrome. (**NOTE:** For additional weight, use a tungsten cone head.) **TAIL:** Black marabou. **BODY:** Peacock herl. **HACKLE:** Grizzly saddle hackle, tied in by the tip.

Midnite Fire Twist Loop Bugger

Here's a novel and very attractive pattern from Buddy Knight of Sandy, Utah. Buddy is a professional guide and fly tier, specializing in still-water designs. I haven't met Buddy, but learned about him through a mutual friend who is familiar with his work. His flies are beautifully tied. Four other Buddy Knight patterns appear in different chapters of the book.

DRESSING

HOOK: Mid-length streamer; Buddy stipulates 4XL; size 6. **THREAD:** Black 6/0. **TAIL:** Black marabou. **ACCENT:** Light blue Flashabou. **RIB:** Black saddle hackle. **BODY:** Buddy's special Midnite Fire dubbing blend, described below.

TYING STEPS, PER BUDDY

1. Tie in the marabou tail.

2. Tie in the accent; one strand only of the light blue Flashabou on each side of the tail.

3. Tie in the hackle feather by the tip end, and strip off all of the fibers from the lower side of the quill. In other words, only half the barbs on the feather will be used.

4. Form a 6-inch dubbing loop and spin on the dubbing.

5. Create ¼ inch of slack in the hackle quill and spin it together with the dubbing. Wrap the body and finish off at the head. A durable assembly is thus created. Then tease out the body by brushing toward the rear with Velcro or a dubbing brush.

TYING NOTES

Dubbing recipe: Mix black Hareline STS Trilobal, a bit of steelie blue Ice Dub, and small amounts of red, purple, and dark blue Flashabou dubbing. This simulates a chenille called New Age Midnite Fire. (Yes, that's how they spell *midnight*.)

WOOLLY BUGGERS (continued)

Woolly Bugger, Brown Dumbbell

Here is another Bugger favorite of mine, shown with the hook inverted, as the dumbbell will cause it to ride that way in the water.

DRESSING

HOOK: Mid-length streamer; here, the 4XL Daiichi model 1750; sizes 4 to 8. **THREAD:** Brown or black 6/0 or 8/0 Uni-Thread or similar. **HEAD:** A dumbbell of your choice. **TAIL:** Brown-dyed grizzly Chickabou or plain brown marabou. **BODY:** Brown chenille. **HACKLE:** Brown saddle or long cape hackle, tied in by the tip.

7

Streamers for the Great Northeast and Beyond

Streamer fly tying and fishing are essentially American. Their development was inspired mainly by the northeastern brook trout and landlocked salmon fishery, as the two species in question are noted carnivores. Many of the patterns are imitations of the landlocked smelt that are abundant throughout the region. These forage fish seem to vary in coloration and size from watershed to watershed; hence the great variety of dressings. Also, there are many so-called attractor patterns that aren't designed to look like any specific baitfish, but rather to appeal to the game fish's penchant for aggressiveness.

Attractor is a convenient term for us anglers, but I doubt that a big, fat brook trout or landlocked salmon goes through a thought process like, "Wow, that's a beautifully tied attractor fly! Guess I should eat it!" To the fish, they are all real and edible fare.

Do these traditional patterns belong in a book that's intended to show and tell what works in today's angling environment? In this case, yes, because we're still fishing for the same species of game fish, and they still take these flies. The brookies and landlocks are native Americans. They've been here since the Ice Age ended, eons before brown trout were brought over from Europe and rainbow trout were hauled east across the continent.

Without breaking with tradition, I've taken the liberty of introducing a few tying techniques and new materials that make it a little quicker and easier to dress these streamers. There are also a few substitutions for expensive or hard-to-find materials, such as jungle cock and Capras goat.

The patterns listed here were contributed by several outstanding angler/tiers who spend a lot of time on the lakes and rivers of the Greater Northeast. These flies are still very much in use and are current favorites of the regulars. I want to express my gratitude to Don Wilson, Ian Cameron, Jim Warner, and Mike Martinek for sharing their expertise.

ORIGINAL BLACK GHOST

This is another of the traditional Maine patterns that still fishes well throughout the Greater Northeast. The originator was Herbert L. Welch of Mooselookmeguntic, Maine.

DRESSING

HOOK: Long streamer, at least 6XL; sizes 2/0 to 6. **THREAD:** Black 6/0 or 8/0 Uni-Thread or similar. **TAIL:** Yellow hackle barbs. **RIB:** Narrow silver tinsel. **BODY:** Black floss. **THROAT:** Yellow hackle barbs. **WING:** Two or four white hackles. **EYES:** Jungle cock.

BLACK GHOST MARABOU

While I've grouped this fly with those patterns essentially intended for northeastern brook trout and landlocked salmon, it's a terrific all-around streamer pattern. I've used it all over North America and in foreign countries on everything from trout to salmon to bass to pike, and it's produced amazingly well. I tie it in a wide range of sizes.

DRESSING

HOOK: Long streamer, at least 6XL; sizes 2 to 8. **THREAD:** Black Uni-Stretch. **TAIL:** Yellow hackle barbs or fine marabou. **RIB:** Narrow silver tinsel. **BODY:** Black Uni-Stretch. **THROAT:** Yellow hackle barbs or fine marabou. **WING:** White marabou plumage. **EYES:** Stick-on or painted-on type, coated with epoxy or some other strong, clear adhesive.

Black Ghost Marabou.

Here, the Black Ghost Marabou is wet, and the marabou compresses.

TYING NOTES

The bobbin-mounted Uni-Stretch is used throughout. It in and of itself builds up the head, which accommodates the eye. If painted eyes are opted for, apply at least one coat of clear head lacquer and let it dry before doing the eyes. Then dot on a white or yellow iris, followed by a black pupil. The rear ends of ¼-inch drill bits work great for this task.

FROST'S BLUE SMELT

This pattern was originated by Dick Frost of Rangeley, Maine, and tied by Don Wilson.

DRESSING

HOOK: Long streamer or connected tandem hooks, as seen in photo; sizes 2 to 8. **THREAD:** Medium blue 8/0 Uni-Thread or similar. **BODY, MAIN AND TRAILER:** Silver braided Mylar tubing tied at the ends with the blue thread. **WING:** White bucktail or calf tail, over which are four strands of peacock herl, over which is a bunch of light blue bucktail or calf tail. **HEAD:** Blue lacquer. **EYES:** Painted white with black pupils.

TYING NOTES

If you can't find blue thread, use white and paint it with the blue water-base enamel found in art and craft stores. A good material for the connector is Tyger Wire, which is flexible coated wire that can be knotted almost as easily as monofilament. Ten-pound test should be sufficient. This protects the connector against strikes from northern pike, which are often found in trout and landlocked salmon lakes. If this is not a concern, ten- to fifteen-pound mono works fine. Bind it securely to the shank of the main hook and apply a coat of superglue or epoxy.

For dotting on the eyes on smaller heads, a round toothpick works well. Cut it in half, and then cut it again halfway down the tapered end: You'll use it to add the pupil. On large heads, the back ends of two small drill bits of different diameters serve the purpose.

CONTEMPORARY GRAY GHOST

Of the ninety-plus patterns originated by Carrie Stevens, the Gray Ghost is the most popular and enduring. The original dressing is still widely used, and it accounts for plenty of sizable trout and salmon every season. Truly, it needs no alteration. With all due reverence, however, I've put together a modified version that's a little easier to tie and considerably less expensive, as there's no jungle cock.

DRESSING

HOOK: Long streamer, at least 6XL; here, the Daiichi model 2370 (which is 7XL); sizes 2 to 8. **THREAD:** First, pumpkin Uni-Stretch, then black 6/0 or 8/0 Uni-Thread or similar. **TAG AND RIB:** Narrow silver tinsel. **BODY:** The pumpkin Uni-Stretch. **UNDERBELLY:** A few strands of peacock herl, below which is a small bunch of white synthetic hair. **UNDERWING:** A few strands of gold flashy material; here, Spectra Splash from Spirit River. **WING:** Two or four medium gray hackles. **CHEEKS:** Silver pheasant, or mallard or teal barred flank feathers. **EYES:** The stick-on type.

TYING NOTES

The pumpkin Uni-Stretch is mounted in a bobbin and is used for both thread and body material in the beginning. Once the body is completed, the Uni-Stretch is tied off, and is replaced with regular tying thread.

The cheek/eye assemblies are prepared beforehand. The eyes are stuck in place, and a very small droplet of glue is placed on the back side of the feather where the eye is located, so that it seeps through and forms a bond. In the past I've used Zap-A-Gap, but I've recently started using plain Elmer's Glue, as it's much easier to control. I also put a tiny bit of it on the very front ends of the cheeking feathers, as this adds durability and helps get them to lie flat against the wings. Elmer's Glue is white, but it dries clear.

If you want to tie this fly really large, you'll need to make a hook substitution, as the one specified above is not available larger than size 2.

JOE'S SMELT

This pattern was originated by Joe Sterling of Danforth, Maine, and tied by Don Wilson.

LAVENDER BADGER SMELT

This is a simple pattern of mine. I was at a winter show and saw this little badger-dyed lavender cape on display. It virtually shouted, "I'm a smelt!" And it was.

DRESSING

HOOK: Long streamer, at least 6XL; here, the 7XL Daiichi model 2370; sizes 2 to 8. **THREAD:** Black 6/0 or 8/0 Uni-Thread or similar. **BODY:** Holographic rainbow tinsel. **BELLY:** White hair, natural or synthetic. **WING:** Four lavender hackles, two fronts and two backs. **COLLAR:** One or two lavender hackles, folded and wrapped.

MAGOG SMELT

This pattern was originated by Fred Gulline and designed for catching landlocked salmon in Lake Memphremagog, which lies partly in Vermont and partly in the province of Quebec.

DRESSING

HOOK: Long streamer, at least 6XL; sizes 2/0 to 6. **THREAD:** Black 6/0 or 8/0 Uni-Thread or similar. **TAIL:** A short bunch of teal barred flank feather. **BODY:** Silver embossed tinsel. **THROAT:** Red hackle barbs. **WING:** White bucktail or calf tail, over which is a bunch of yellow bucktail or calf tail, over which is a larger bunch of purple bucktail or calf tail, topped by five or six strands of peacock herl. **CHEEKS:** Teal barred flank feathers, about one-third the length of the wing. **EYES:** Jungle cock "nails."

TYING NOTES

Jungle cock is legally available, but expensive. An acceptable substitute can be formed by cutting around a white dot centered on a guinea fowl feather quill. Refer to the tying steps for the Hornberg in the General Streamers chapter.

MELVIN BAY

This pattern was contributed by Ian Cameron, outstanding Maine guide and bon vivant.

> **DRESSING**
>
> **HOOK:** Long streamer, at least 6XL; here, the Mike Martinek hook, produced by Gaelic Supreme; sizes 2 to 8. **THREAD:** Black 6/0 or 8/0 Uni-Thread or similar. **RIB:** Medium oval tinsel. **BODY:** Flat silver tinsel. **THROAT:** Red hackle barbs. **WING:** A sparse bunch of yellow bucktail, over which is a sparse bunch of red bucktail, over which is a bunch of gray marabou. **HIGHLIGHT (OPTIONAL):** Six strands of either red or yellow Krystal Flash. **TOPPING:** Six strands of peacock herl. **CHEEKS:** Teal barred flank feathers, about one-third the length of the wing.

PHANTOM SMELT

This pattern was originated by Bob Upham of Grand Lake Stream, Maine, and tied by Don Wilson.

DRESSING

HOOK: Long streamer, at least 6XL; sizes 2 to 8. **THREAD:** Black 6/0 or 8/0 Uni-Thread or similar. **BODY:** Silver diamond braid. **THROAT/BELLY:** White bucktail the length of the hook. **WING:** From the bottom: six strands of clear Crystal Hair (or Krystal Flash), six strands of orange Crystal Hair (or Krystal Flash), and six strands of peacock Crystal Hair (or Krystal Flash), topped by a sparse bunch of gray bucktail, over which are a few strands of gray ostrich herl.

TYING NOTES

There are a number of similar flashy materials that bear the name Crystal, or Krystal. In my opinion, they may be used interchangeably. Bob Upham, the originator of this pattern, says that a smelt fly should be sparse enough to read a newspaper through. I encourage readers to apply a little latitude to that statement. He recommends fast-trolling this fly.

RED-GRAY GHOST

One of my primary consultants on flies for Maine and the Greater Northeast, including Canada, is Ian Cameron, the noted Maine guide. He tells us that brook trout like red, and recommends a standard pattern, the Red-Gray Ghost. I have taken the dressing, as tied by Mike Martinek, from the Dick Stewart and Farrow Allen book, *Flies for Trout*.

> **DRESSING**
>
> **HOOK:** Long streamer; here, the 8XL model of the Mike Martinek Rangeley Streamer hook; sizes 2/0 to 6. **THREAD:** First, Chinese red Uni-Stretch, then black 6/0 or 8/0 Uni-Thread or similar. **TAG AND RIB:** Narrow silver tinsel. **BODY:** The Chinese red Uni-Stretch. **UNDERBELLY/ THROAT:** A bunch of red bucktail, then one or two golden pheasant crests, then a bunch of red hackle barbs. **UNDERWING:** Four or five strands of peacock herl.

THE ULTIMATE SMELT SERIES

This series of simple yet elegant smelt streamers represents the expertise of Mike Martinek. The streamers are consistent with two of the main considerations of smelt pattern design: sparseness and translucency. The synthetic hair chosen for the wings produces such an effect admirably. The flies shown here were tied by the designer himself. They have proven to be very effective on the northern New England lakes that Mike frequents.

The Mike Martinek Rangeley Streamer hook is imported from England by the Belvoirdale Company. (Somehow, that's pronounced "Beaverdale.") The 8XL model was used for the flies shown here. A 10XL model is also available, which seems a bit extreme to me, but if all you do is troll, it might be practical.

Note that the wings on these streamers barely reach beyond the rear of the hook. This is enabled by the longer shank and helps prevent the materials from getting wrapped around the hook bend.

Ultimate Smelt, Green

DRESSING

HOOK: Long streamer; here, the 8XL model of the Mike Martinek Rangeley Streamer hook; sizes 1/0 to 4. **THREAD:** 6/0 Danville Flymaster, 8/0 Uni-Thread, or similar. **BODY:** Pearl curling ribbon, divided lengthwise to desired width. **BELLY:** 70-denier Fishair, in the color known as polar bear. **WING:** In layers starting from the bottom: smoke-colored Super Hair, a few strands of pearl DNA Holoflash synthetic hair, a few strands of pale orchid Unique Hair, all topped with dark green Unique Hair. **EYES:** Stick-on type.

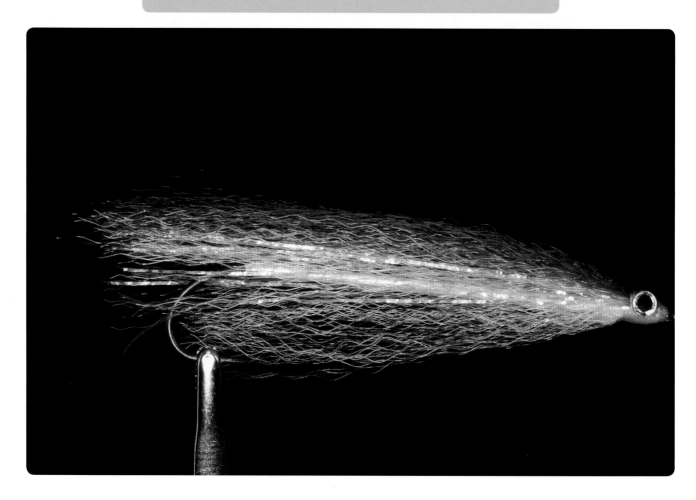

THE ULTIMATE SMELT SERIES (continued)

Ultimate Smelt, Olive

DRESSING

HOOK: Long streamer; here, the 8XL model of the Mike Martinek Rangeley Streamer hook; sizes 1 and 2. **THREAD:** 6/0 Danville Flymaster, 8/0 Uni-Thread, or similar. **BODY:** Pearl curling ribbon, divided lengthwise to desired width. **BELLY:** 70-denier Fishair, in the color known as polar bear. **WING:** In layers starting from the bottom: smoke-colored Super Hair, a few strands of pearl DNA Holoflash synthetic hair, a few strands of orchid Unique Hair topped with olive Unique Hair. **EYES:** Stick-on type.

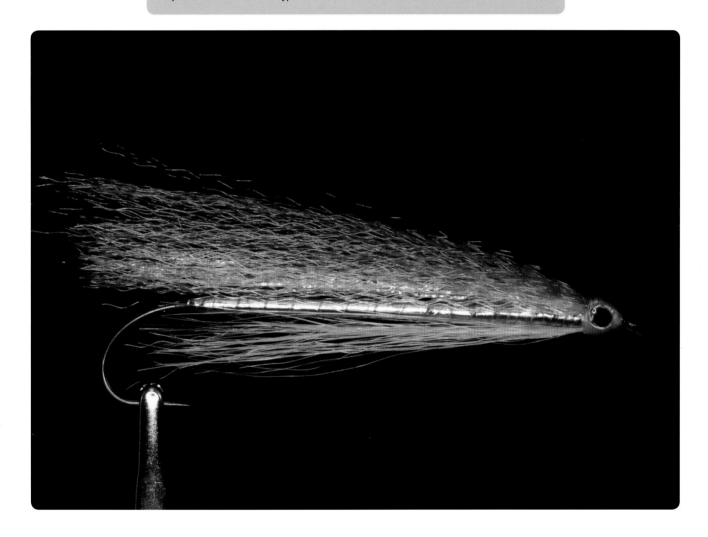

THE ULTIMATE SMELT SERIES (continued)

Ultimate Smelt, Purple

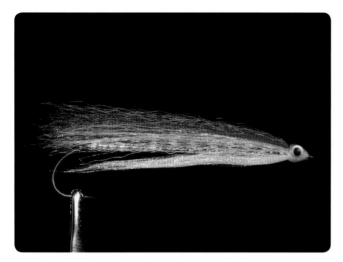

Ultimate Smelt, Rose

DRESSING

HOOK: Long streamer; here, the 8XL model of the Mike Martinek Rangeley Streamer hook; sizes 1 and 2. **THREAD:** 6/0 Danville Flymaster, 8/0 Uni-Thread, or similar. **BODY:** Rose-colored curling ribbon, divided lengthwise to desired width and over-wrapped with transparent holographic pearl Mylar tinsel. **BELLY:** 70-denier Fishair, in the color known as polar bear. **WING:** In layers starting from the bottom: smoke-colored Super Hair, a few strands of pearl DNA Holoflash synthetic hair, a few strands of magenta Unique Hair, then purple Unique Hair topped with gray Unique Hair. **EYES:** Stick-on type.

DRESSING

HOOK: Long streamer; here, the 8XL model of the Mike Martinek Rangeley Streamer hook; sizes 1 and 2. **THREAD:** 6/0 Danville Flymaster, 8/0 Uni-Thread, or similar. **BODY:** Purple-colored curling ribbon, divided lengthwise to desired width and over-wrapped with transparent holographic pearl Mylar tinsel. **BELLY:** 70-denier Fishair, in the color known as polar bear. **WING:** In layers starting from the bottom: smoke-colored Super Hair, a few strands of pearl DNA Holoflash synthetic hair, rose-colored Unique Hair, all topped with gray Unique Hair. **EYES:** Stick-on type.

TYING NOTES

Unique Hair and Super Hair are similar. Mike recommends using Super Hair for the lower layer of the wing, as it's slightly stiffer. The curling ribbon is found in practically any craft or party store. It comes in a number of colors, is very easy to work with, and is also very durable. The bodies are also coated with a clear lacquer.

WILSON JR.

This pattern was originated by Alfred J. Wilson Jr. of Moosehead Lake, Maine, and tied by Don Wilson.

WINNIPESAUKEE SMELT

The fly seen here was tied by the originator, Jim Warner, of Wolfeboro, New Hampshire.

DRESSING

HOOK: Long streamer, at least 6XL; Jim specifies the Carrie Stevens model in size 4. **THREAD:** Black 6/0 or 8/0 Uni-Thread or similar. **BODY:** Wide flat silver tinsel; a double layer, heavily lacquered. **WING:** Sparse white bucktail, then three or four strands of peacock herl, then a small bunch of lavender-dyed Capras hair or a substitute (see tying notes), then a single white marabou plume that has little or no quill. **TOPPING:** One or two blue/black crest feathers from a silver pheasant. **EYES:** Pearlescent paint or lacquer, with a black pupil.

TYING NOTES

The Capras is a breed of goat. The natural color of the hair is white, and it is long and fairly soft. It takes dyes very well. Fine, straight, soft bucktail may be substituted, as may other hairs with similar characteristics.

— 8 —

Special and Novel Patterns

THE BLUE WONDER

Here's another Buddy Knight pattern. The photographed fly is one he sent me. Exactly what it imitates, I'm not sure, but the fish love it, and that's the bottom line.

DRESSING

HOOK: 2XL nymph; Daiichi model 1710 or similar; size 12. **THREAD:** Black 8/0 Uni-Thread or similar. **HEAD:** A 1/8-ounce bead. **TAIL:** Pale blue Poly Marabou. **RIB:** Fine blue wire. **BODY:** Peacock herl. **LEGS:** Blue rubber leg material. **WING:** Pale blue Poly Marabou. **HACKLE:** Brown hen.

TYING STEPS, PER BUDDY

1. Slide on the bead and mount the hook in the vise.
2. Wrap on ten turns of the weighting wire and push it forward against the rear of the bead.
3. Tie in a 2-inch piece of red Antron that is half the thickness desired for the tail. Tie it in by the middle at the center of the hook, to the rear of the wire. Wrap to the rear, covering the yarn, then double it back and wrap forward.
4. Tie in the ribbing wire.
5. Tie in four peacock herls, wrap them forward, and tie them off. Then wrap the rib.
6. Tie in a piece of the wing material twice as long as the finished wing will be, and half the thickness. Tie it in behind the bead by the middle. Then tie in by the centers two 1½-inch strips of rubber leg material, one on each side of the hook. Double the wing yarn and tie it down.
7. Strip off the barbs from one side of the hen hackle, tie it in by the tip, and wrap only one turn. This finishes the fly.

CHERNOBYL ANT

This is one more example of the growing popularity of closed-cell foam as a dry-fly material. The sample was sent by The Fly Shop of Redding. It is tied in a number of colors, and you can make up some more, if you wish. I've listed the components generically as closed-cell foam, but the easiest way to prepare these flies is to buy the preformed bodies, which are generally available in fly shops in a variety of color combinations.

DRESSING

HOOK: Long-shanked dry fly; Daiichi model 1280, 2460, or comparable; large sizes, 2 to 6. **THREAD:** Yellow 6/0 or 8/0 Uni-Thread or similar. **BODY, FIRST LAYER:** Tan closed-cell foam sheet, trimmed to shape (see tying notes). **BODY, SECOND LAYER:** Tan closed-cell foam sheet, trimmed to the same shape as the **FIRST** layer. **REAR LEGS:** Tan rubber leg material, one strip on each side of the body. **REAR HIGHLIGHT:** A small block of orange closed-cell foam, tied on concurrent with the legs. **FRONT LEGS:** Tan rubber leg material, one strip on each side of the body **FRONT HIGHLIGHT:** A small block of white closed-cell foam, tied on concurrent with the legs.

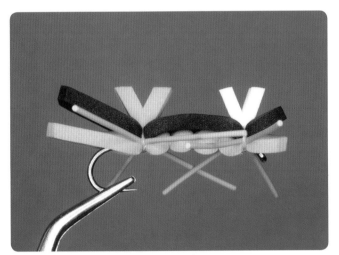

Side view.

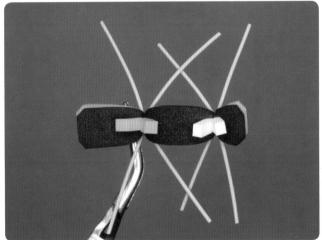

Top view.

TYING NOTES

As stated, if you prefer not to get involved with cutting the foam to shape, you can buy Chernobyl Ant bodies all set to go, in several colors and sizes.

DEAD DRIFT CRAYFISH

This is Tim Haddon's Dead Drift Crayfish. It's hard to beat crustaceans for fish food, and this pattern is both tie-able and effective. It will take bass and steelhead as well as trout. Tim has enjoyed great success with it all over the West, including on his home river, the Truckee. I'm looking forward to my first trip to Chile this coming winter, and I'm sure this pattern will work wonderfully well as an imitation of the Chilean crayfish, the pancora.

> **DRESSING**
>
> **HOOK:** Tiemco model 5263; size 8. **THREAD:** Black 6/0. **MOUTH PARTS:** A tuft of orange rabbit fur. **ANTENNAE:** Pheasant tail fibers and two strands of orange Krystal Flash. **EYES:** Small silver bead chain. **CLAWS:** Two pieces of rabbit strip, the color being gold variant. **CARAPACE:** Wapsi Thin Skin, labeled Mottled Bustard Orange. **RIB:** Fine black Ultrawire. **HACKLE:** Brown saddle. **BODY:** Wapsi Sow Scud dubbing, olive.

Top view.

Bottom view.

GARTSIDE'S GURGLER

This is another of Jack Gartside's unique and productive designs. Its action on the surface makes it irresistible to quite a variety of game fish. It is tied in a number of colors and sizes. The most important ingredient is, of course, the closed-cell foam. This can be purchased in fly shops and elsewhere. Craft stores, such as Michael's, have lots of useful foam products. To float properly, the foam needs to be at least ⅛ inch thick. The width to which you cut the strip will vary a little, depending on the diameter of the hook shank and the thickness of the hair underbody. The strip seen here is ⁷⁄₁₆ inch wide. This allows it to encircle the hook and underbody.

DRESSING

(BASIC WHITE)

HOOK: Medium to long-shanked; here, the 4XL Daiichi model 1750; sizes 4 to 8. **THREAD:** Something strong, such as the white Uni-Nylon 210-denier seen here. **TAIL:** White bucktail or similar hair. **HIGHLIGHT:** Pearl Krystal Flash, Glimmer, or similar. **BODY/BACK:** A strip of white closed-cell foam about two and a half times the shank length. **HACKLE:** A somewhat webby long white saddle or neck hackle.

NOTE: The Gurgler is also tied for saltwater fishing. For this, I recommend a chromed saltwater hook with a fairly long shank. My favorite is the Daiichi model X472, 3XL, in sizes 2/0 to 2.

TYING STEPS

1. Cover the hook shank with thread. Tie in the tail hair near the eye of the hook and cover it as an underbody, wrapping the thread to the bend. Then tie in the flash material and double it rearward.

2. Cut a strip of the foam about two and a half times the shank length.

TYING STEPS continued

GARTSIDE'S GURGLER (continued)

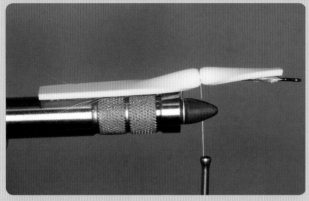

3. Tie in the foam strip at the very bend of the hook with the front of it extending nearly to the hook eye.

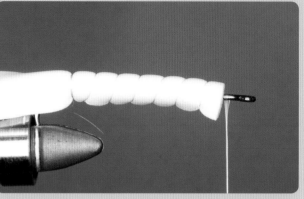

4. Now grip the foam so that it encircles the hook and spiral-wrap the thread around it, working toward the eye, regripping the foam with each progressive turn and spacing the wraps so that you'll end up with five to seven turns.

5. Tie off the thread, go back to the bend where the first encircling wrap was made, and tie on again. Tie in the hackle feather by the tip end, and wrap the thread forward to near the eye, following the first set of spiral wraps. Then wrap the hackle, also following the spirals, and tie it off. You can trim off the topmost barbs if you wish, but it's not mandatory, as they will be buried with the next step.

6. Bend the remainder of the foam strip forward and take a half-dozen or so firm thread wraps around the "neck" of the fly, causing the foam to encircle the hook. Finish the fly by bringing half the strands of flash material forward over the back and tying it off. Also, cut the "lip" of foam to the desired length.

TYING NOTES

The reason that I tie off after making the first set of spiral wraps, then tie back on at the bend, is that I want to avoid crushing the foam by spiral-wrapping rearward to where the hackle will be attached.

THE GURGULATOR

The Gurgulator is an innovation of mine. It borrows from both the Gartside's Gurgler and the ever-popular Stimulator, and it also incorporates several innovations. It serves as both an effective imitation of a number of insects, both aquatic and terrestrial, and a great indicator fly. Moderately weighted nymphs, such as the PTBT Nymphs shown in this book, can be suspended below the Gurgulator.

DRESSING

HOOK: Long-shanked dry fly; here, the 4XL Daiichi model 2460; sizes 8 and 10 (see tying notes). **THREAD:** Something strong, such as the white Uni-Nylon 210-denier seen here. **TAIL:** Deer body hair. **BODY/BACK:** A strip of yellow closed-cell foam about two and a half times the shank length. **HACKLE:** A grizzly dry-fly-grade saddle feather with a fairly short barb. (**NOTE:** The hackle barbs should be only about as long as the hook gape. This gives the fly better balance on the water.) **WING:** Deer body hair. **ADHESIVE:** Superglue, such as Zap-A-Gap or Plastic Surgery, which is produced by a company named SureHold and is sold in hardware stores by that name.

TYING STEPS

1. Cover the hook shank with thread. Tie in the tail hair about a quarter of the shank length rearward of the hook eye and cover it as an underbody, wrapping the thread to the bend. The tail should be quite short, as shown.

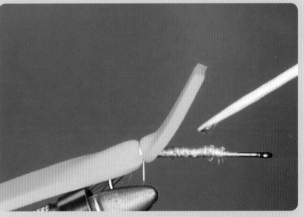

2. Tie in the foam strip at the very bend of the hook. At this point, it's a good idea to fold back the foam strip and cover the thread wraps with a thin coating of superglue. The emphasis is on *thin*; you don't want this stuff oozing out onto your fingers.

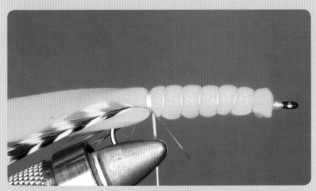

3. Follow the instructions for the Gurgler, forming the segmented foam body. Tie off, go back to the bend, tie on again, and tie in the hackle feather, this time by the butt end.

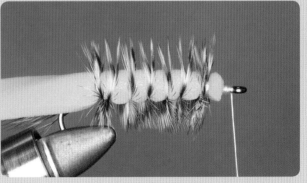

4. Wrap the thread forward to near the eye, following the spirals. Hen-wrap the hackle, also following the spirals, with the "pretty" side of the feather facing forward.

TYING STEPS continued

THE GURGULATOR (continued)

5. Bend the remainder of the foam strip forward and tie it down using plenty of thread wraps, so as to create a base for the wing. Then tie in a bundle of deer hair and trim the butts. The wing should extend to slightly beyond the end of the foam body and should be fairly sparse.

6. Finish the fly by bringing the remaining foam back over the wing butts and tying it down. This will spread and reposition the wing. Tie off, then trim the excess foam from around the head. I like to use an orange permanent marker to simulate the orange thorax of the Stimulator, but this is optional. Coat the finishing thread wraps with superglue.

TYING NOTES

The Daiichi model 2460 hook specified above is listed as a streamer hook. However, the wire is light enough for tying long-bodied dry flies, such as the Gurgulator. This particular bronze-finish hook is not available larger than size 8. However, for different-sized Gurgulators, it is available in larger sizes in a black finish as the model 2461. Other hooks may also be used to achieve varying effects, such as 2XL and 3XL dry-fly models. For really large versions, fairly light-wire streamer hooks will work, including the Daiichi 2461. The so-called stinger hooks also work fine when a wider gape is desired.

7. A top view.

Gurgulator Hopper

Same as the original, except for the two-tone colors. Yellow and green are shown here, but feel free to substitute other colors to match your local hoppers.

Gurgulator Cricket

Same as the original, but all black.

Gurgulator Salmon Fly

This dressing imitates the great western stonefly, *Pteronarcys californica*. Same as the original, but with orange foam, brown hackle, and a proportionately larger hook.

Gurgulator Salmon Fly RL

Same as Gurgulator Salmon Fly, but with optional rubber legs added.

Gurgulator Beetle

Same as the Cricket, but with no wing or tail.

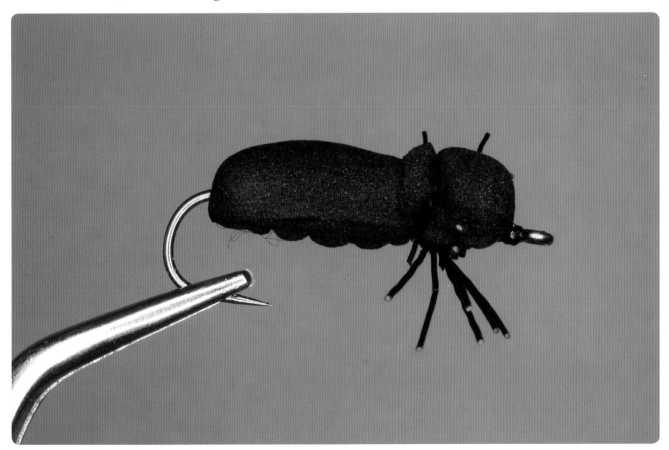

LITHUANIAN BAT

I've made three trips to Alaska, and each time the Lithuanian Bat was the most productive all-around fly in my arsenal. All of the Alaska species went for it: the rainbow trout, the char, the sea-run Dolly Vardens, the silver salmon—all of them. It's also a very good bass and catfish fly. Yes, catfish can be caught on a fly—ask Bob Clouser. I also tie it in purple.

DRESSING

HOOK: Medium-length substantial hook; here, a Daiichi salmon hook, model 2421; sizes 2 and 4. If you wish to tie this fly larger, select a substitute hook, as size 2 is the largest available for the one specified. **THREAD:** Black Uni-Stretch or similar. **HEAD:** A dumbbell. **TAIL:** A straight-cut strip of black rabbit. **COLLAR:** A cross-cut strip of black rabbit. **FINISHING FILL-IN MATERIAL:** Black yarn.

TYING STEPS

1. Tie on the dumbbell with X-wraps, then wrap to the hook bend and tie on the tailing strip.

2. Tie in the cross-cut rabbit strip and wrap it collar-style, finishing at the rear of the dumbbell.

3. Finish the fly by filling up the space in the center of the dumbbell with X-wraps of yarn.

HEAVY-HOOKED MADAM X

In The Fly Shop of Redding catalog, I noticed a pattern called the Heavy-Hooked Madam X. I asked them to send me a sample, and saw that it was tied on a standard-wire, up-eyed salmon hook. I would imagine this hook was chosen with steelhead in mind. For trout fishing, a lighter hook could be substituted, perhaps the Bob Veverka dry-fly salmon hook, Daiichi model 2131; or any 2XL to 4XL medium- to light-wire hook.

> **DRESSING**
>
> **HOOK:** Typical low-water salmon fly; Daiichi model 2421 or comparable; sizes 2 to 8. **THREAD:** Fairly heavy; yellow 3/0 Uni-Thread or similar. **TAIL:** Deer or elk body hair, tied short. **BODY:** Tying thread. **WING:** Deer or elk body hair, tied in extending off the front of the hook, then drawn back and tied down bullet-head-style. **LEGS:** White rubber leg material, one strip on each side of the body.

Side view.

Bottom view.

MINI TIGER BEETLE

This is another fly from Blue Ribbon Flies. They've found that small terrestrials like this one are often more effective than the larger and ever-popular grasshopper and cricket patterns. The bright stripe down the back imbues this low-floater with greatly enhanced visibility.

DRESSING

HOOK: Tiemco 102Y or similar; size 19. **THREAD:** BRF didn't specify, so I suggest black. **SHELL (BACK):** Mini Tiger foam strip. **BODY:** Black Zelon dubbing **LEGS:** Bug leg material.

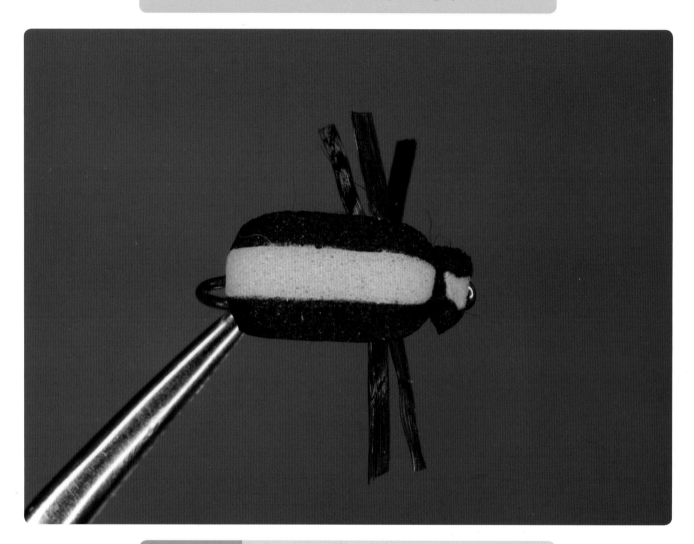

TYING NOTES

Mini Tiger material is a black closed-cell foam with a stripe down the center. The one seen here has an orange stripe, but it comes in other colors. The foam strip is tied in upside-down and hanging to the rear, and is brought forward over the body at the very end and tied off. The bug legs are just what they sound like, and the material is sold in fly shops. The Zelon dubbing is shiny and fine, and it's fairly easy to work with. These materials are all available from Blue Ribbon Flies and other fine stores.

TWO FINE MICE

Mouse patterns are great for attracting large game fish of many species. I have chosen two outstanding examples for inclusion in the book: the Mouse-Rat and the Morrish Mouse. The latter was designed by Ken Morrish, a noted guide and teacher of fly fishing.

I found that the deer hair I had on hand wasn't well-suited to mouse-tying, so I consulted one of hair-tying's true mavens, Chris Helm. Chris is the proprietor of Whitetail Fly Tieing Supplies (yes, that's the way he spells it). If you're looking for the right hair for whatever fly you might be working on, consult with Chris. He'll make sure that what you get works for the size and type of fly at hand.

I bought two different lengths of hair, as shown in the photograph: the longer hair for the Mouse-Rat, the shorter for the Morrish. This is important, because in order for the hair to be spun or stacked, the thread must intercept it in the butt portion, where it is softer and on the "pulpy" side.

The other critical component is the thread. You'll want gel-spun, also known as gel thread, or simply GSP. I'm using Uni-Cord 100-denier, formerly listed as 7/0.

Longer hairs for the Mouse-Rat, shorter hairs for the Morrish Mouse.

Mouse-Rat

DRESSING

HOOK: Medium shank length; here, the 4XL Daiichi model 1750; size 4. **THREAD:** A gel thread; here, Uni-Cord 100-denier. **TAIL:** A narrow, tapered piece of either suede or Chuck Furimsky's Bugskin. **BODY:** The longer of the two deer hairs shown in the photo. **ADHESIVE:** A superglue, such as Zap-A-Gap or Plastic Surgery, produced by SureHold and sold in hardware stores by that name.

TYING STEPS

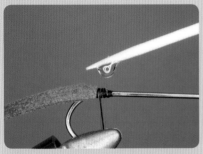

1. Wrap a small thread base at the rear of the hook, tie the tail in place, and apply a small droplet of superglue. Be sure the glue is absolutely dry before continuing.

2. For a better-looking mouse, use a stacker to even up the tips of the hair.

3. Spin or stack the hair in place. It will hide the tail tie-on.

4. Secure the hair with several very firm thread wraps directly on top of the first ones. Then slide the thread forward through the hair butts and use a packing tool to concentrate the bunch. Hold on to the hair with your left hand while doing this. Repeat this step until the hook eye is reached.

5. When all of the hair bunches have been secured, tie off and trim the bottom flat, using a razor blade or scissors. Then saturate the trimmed hairs with superglue.

6. The finished Mouse-Rat.

TYING NOTES

An alternate choice for a hook is the so-called stinger type, commonly used in bass-bug tying. Either suede or Bugskin is recommended for the tail, because plain leather stiffens after it gets wet and becomes brittle.

TWO FINE MICE (continued)

Morrish Mouse

DRESSING

HOOK: Medium shank length; here, the Daiichi model 1750; size 4. **THREAD:** A gel thread; here, Uni-Cord 100-denier. **TAIL:** A narrow, tapered piece of either suede or Chuck Furimsky's Bugskin. **BACK:** A strip of thick, black closed-cell foam, cut to the shape shown. **BODY:** The shorter of the two deer hairs shown in the photo. **ADHESIVE:** A superglue, such as Zap-A-Gap or Plastic Surgery, produced by SureHold and sold in hardware stores by that name.

TYING STEPS

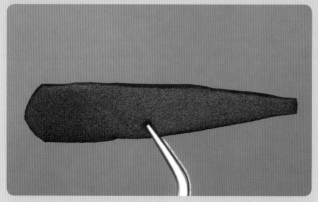

1. This is how the foam for the Morrish Mouse back piece is shaped.

2. First, tie on a tail as was shown for the Mouse-Rat. Then the back piece is tied in extending to the rear. It will be folded over the back after all the hair has been tied on. Continue per the Mouse-Rat instructions.

3. The finished Morrish Mouse.

TYING NOTES

Most fly shops carry a good selection of closed-cell foam products. However, if you can't find what you're looking for, go to a craft store, such as Michael's. There you'll find a wide array of foam products.

SAN JUAN WORMS

This pattern apparently originated on the San Juan River, a tailrace fishery in northern New Mexico. The more persnickety fly fishers among us tend to denigrate it, saying it's not a fly, per se. But I can tell you this: It's an imitation of a natural trout food. There actually is a semiaquatic worm that lives in the soggy soil of the river banks out West. I've dug them up for observation, and they look like small night crawlers.

I can also assure you that this fly is very effective, and has turned around some slow days for me. They are tied in several styles and in as many colors as there are of the special chenille used to tie them. I found in my visits to the San Juan that every season the shops featured a new color of the worm that was an *absolute must* for that year. And if you'd like to buy a bridge to Brooklyn . . .

Red San Juan Worm

My first encounter with the San Juan Worm was on the Bighorn River, a tailrace fishery in southeastern Montana. It was red, and it worked just dandy. Here's how I tie it.

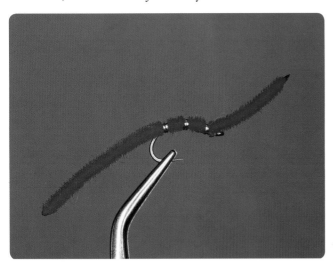

DRESSING

HOOK: Typical nymph/scud hook; here, the Daiichi model 1150; size 14. **THREAD:** Red 8/0 Uni-Thread or similar. **WORM MATERIAL:** Red Ultra Chenille or Vernille. **RIB:** Fine gold oval tinsel; three turns only, covering the thread wraps.

TYING NOTES

After tying on the chenille, tie in the tinsel in the same spot. Take two wraps of tinsel, over the thread wraps. Now lift up the front of the chenille and advance the thread a few turns, binding down the tinsel as you go. Take a second set of wraps over the tinsel and again cover them with two turns of the tinsel. Repeat the previous step, making a third set of thread and tinsel wraps. Lift the chenille and whip-finish.

Pink San Juan Worm

Why pink? Beats me, but it's been a day-saver for me on more than one occasion.

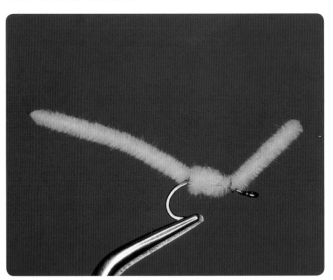

DRESSING

HOOK: Typical nymph/scud hook; here, the Daiichi model 1150; size 14. **THREAD:** Red 8/0 Uni-Thread or similar. **WORM MATERIAL:** Pink Ultra Chenille or Vernille.

TYING NOTES

This is a very simple worm. I tie in the chenille at the bend and advance the thread to where I want to tie off. I then wrap the chenille around the hook a few times, tie it off, and whip-finish.

GARTSIDE'S SPARROW

This is one of Jack Gartside's best-known patterns. It's been around for some time, and for good reason: It's deadly. I think it epitomizes Jack's approach to fly design: He uses materials that look alive in the water and tying techniques that enhance freedom of movement. Trout eat living things, and that's what this fly looks like. With the exception of the body, all components come from a cock ringneck pheasant.

DRESSING

HOOK: Wet fly/nymph; here, the 1XL Daiichi model 1560; sizes 6 to 10. **THREAD:** Camel or brown 8/0 Uni-Thread or similar. **TAIL:** Dark pheasant marabou from the bird's rump. **BODY:** Hare's ear dubbing mix, with some sparkly stuff mixed in, if you wish. **HACKLE:** A pheasant saddle feather. **HEAD:** One or two pheasant aftershaft plumes, wrapped.

Evening (Dark) Sparrow

This is a dark version of the Sparrow.

DRESSING

HOOK: Wet fly/nymph; here, the 1XL Daiichi model 1560; sizes 6 to 10. **THREAD:** Black 8/0 Uni-Thread or similar. **TAIL:** Dark pheasant marabou from the bird's rump. **BODY:** Peacock herl. **HACKLE:** A pheasant saddle feather, dyed black. **HEAD:** One or two pheasant aftershaft plumes, dyed black and wrapped.

STRIKE INDICATOR FLY

This unique pattern came to me from The Fly Shop of Redding, a store that carries an enormous inventory of flies. It reminds me of my first experience with strike indicators on a float trip down the Bighorn River. Trout were hitting the indicator as often as they were the nymph I had on, and I silently wondered if perhaps a hook should be embedded in it.

DRESSING

HOOK: 2XL TMC 5212 dry fly or similar, here shown in size 8. **THREAD:** Yellow or red 6/0 or 8/0 Uni-Thread. **BODY:** Yellow or orange closed-cell foam, 2mm thick, cut to shape. **WING/HEAD:** Red and yellow polypropylene yarn, such as macramé yarn. **LEGS:** Brown rubber leg material, one strand on each side.

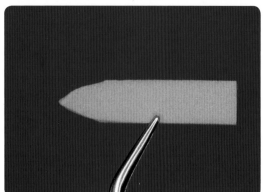

This is how the foam piece is shaped for the Strike Indicator Fly.

TYING NOTES

The bunches of yarn are tied on extending forward over the hook eye, and are then folded back and tied down bullet-head-style.

TURCK'S TARANTULAS

This trademarked fly is the creation of one Guy Turck, and has won international acclaim. It's not hard to tie, but takes a little getting used to. The only problem I originally had was that I inadvertently cut off one of the rubber legs on each of the first three. That got my attention, and I have learned to be careful when trimming the deer hair.

Golden Turck's Tarantula

For our "study" fly, here's the Golden Turck's Tarantula.

> **DRESSING**
>
> **HOOK:** 3XL or 4XL; here, the Daiichi model 2460; sizes 8 and 10. **THREAD:** Start with beige or yellow 8/0 Uni-Thread or similar, then switch to a gel thread. **TAIL:** Golden pheasant tippet strands. **BODY:** Light-colored hare's ear mixed with yellow rabbit fur. **WING:** White calf tail. **WING TOPPING:** Pearl Krystal Flash or similar. **COLLAR:** Light-colored natural or golden-colored deer hair. **LEGS:** Brown or yellow rubber leg material, two legs (one strip) on each side. **HEAD:** Same as for the collar.

TYING STEPS

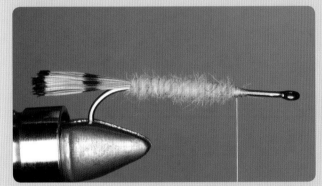

1. Cover the rear two-thirds of the hook with thread and tie the tail.

2. Dub the body, using the spinning loop method, and tie on the wing and topping. Then tie off with the regular thread and tie on with gel-spun thread.

3. Clean and stack a small bunch of the hair. Position it so that the tips reach about halfway down the body, no more than that. Cut off the hair butts immediately ahead of the hook eye. Then make three very firm thread wraps, one on top of the other, flaring the hair. This is stacking, so hold the hair in place as you tighten.

4. On either side of the hook, lay in a piece of rubber leg material and make one or two more firm wraps, drawing the legs in with the hair. Hold on to the hair collar during this procedure so it stays put. Pass the thread through the hair butts, stand up the hair, and wrap to the eye and back.

TYING STEPS continued

TURCK'S TARANTULAS (continued)

5. Clean and spin on another small bunch of hair, allowing it to encircle the hook this time. Secure it, pass the thread to the front, pack the hair with your fingers, and tie a whip finish.

6. Trim the head with great care, holding the legs away from the cutting area.

7. A top view, showing the deployment of the legs.

TYING NOTES

Back when we were spinning deer hair with thread that resembled the mooring line of the *QE2*, the rule was to spin over bare hook. With gel thread, that's no longer the case; in fact, a much more durable result is obtained by spinning over a layer or two of the thread. Here, I'm using a very fine-denier gel thread, the Uni-Cord 50-denier, which prior to the change in thread designations was labeled 12/0. For smaller hair work, this thread is ideal, as it takes up so little space. However, heavier deniers will work okay.

As mentioned in the tying steps, I recommend using the spinning loop technique for dubbing the bodies on Turck's Tarantulas. The size of the flies and the amount of dubbing required makes this a good choice. Also, it produces a much tighter-packed body, which is desirable on a dry fly.

As mentioned earlier in the book, the Daiichi model 2460 comes no larger than a size 8. For larger flies, you might use the Daiichi model 2461, which has a black finish, or any other light-wire long-shanked hook.

If you need further detail on the collar/head assembly, try to get your hands on a copy of the May 2006 *Fly Fisherman Magazine*. On page 45 you'll find a photo sequence by Chris Helm, who is an excellent hair tier.

Original Turck's Tarantula

I believe this is the first dressing for this fly.

DRESSING

HOOK: 3XL or 4XL; here, the Daiichi 4XL model 2460; sizes 4 to 8.
THREAD: Start with camel or brown 8/0 Uni-Thread or similar, then switch to a gel thread. **TAIL:** Golden pheasant tippet strands. **BODY:** Hare's ear. **WING:** White calf tail. **WING TOPPING:** Pearl Krystal Flash or similar. **COLLAR:** Natural deer hair. **LEGS:** Brown rubber leg material, two legs (one strip) on each side. **HEAD:** Same as for the collar.

Red Turck's Tarantula

The Red Turck's Tarantula was suggested to me by my Maine connection, guide Ian Cameron. He says the brookies and landlocks love it, as do the bass.

Side view.

Bottom view.

DRESSING

HOOK: 3XL or 4XL; here, the Daiichi model 2460. Refer to notes following the Golden Turck's Tarantula for hook size information. **THREAD:** Start with red 8/0 Uni-Thread or similar, then switch to a gel thread. **TAIL:** Amherst pheasant tippet strands. **BODY:** Red-dyed hare's ear mix. **WING:** White calf tail. **WING TOPPING:** Pearl Krystal Flash or similar. **COLLAR:** Light-colored natural deer hair. **LEGS:** White rubber leg material, two legs (one strip) on each side. **HEAD:** Same as for the collar.

BIBLIOGRAPHY

Ames, Thomas Jr. *Hatch Guide for New England Streams*. Frank Amato Publications, Inc., 2000.

Bates, Joseph D. Jr. *Streamer Fly Tying and Fishing*. Stackpole Company, 1950 and 1966.

Flick, Arthur B. *New Streamside Guide to Naturals and Their Imitations*. Crown Publishers, 1972.

Gartside, Jack. *Fly Patterns for the Adventurous Tyer,* 4th edition (self-published).

Hilyard, Graydon R., and Leslie K. Hilyard. *Carrie Stevens*. Stackpole Books, 2000.

Lafontaine, Gary. *Caddisflies*. Nick Lyons Books, 1981.

Leiser, Eric. *The Book of Fly Patterns*. Alfred A. Knopf, Inc., 1987.

Soucie, Gary. *Woolly Wisdom.* Frank Amato Publications, 2005

Stuart, Dick, and Farrow Allen. *Flies for Trout*. Mountain Pond Publishing, 1993.

Talleur, Dick. *Inside Fly Tying*. Stackpole Books, 2004.

Wilson, Donald A. *Smelt Fly Patterns*. Frank Amato Publications, 1996.

———. *Wilson Fly Patterns*. Flyfishing University, 2005.

INDEX

ABOUT THE AUTHOR

Dick Talleur has long been considered one of the most authoritative and genuinely effective fly-tying teachers in the world. Talleur has created numerous original patterns that are now in regular production, having worked as a consultant for and professional tyer in the fly-tying industry. He is the author of *The Versatile Fly Tyer*, *Modern Fly-Tying Materials*, *Talleur's Basic Fly Tying*, and the *L.L. Bean Fly Tying Handbook*. Talleur currently writes a regular column for *American Angler* and *Fly Tyer* magazines. He has fly-fished extensively across the western hemisphere and abroad, and he lives in North Carolina.

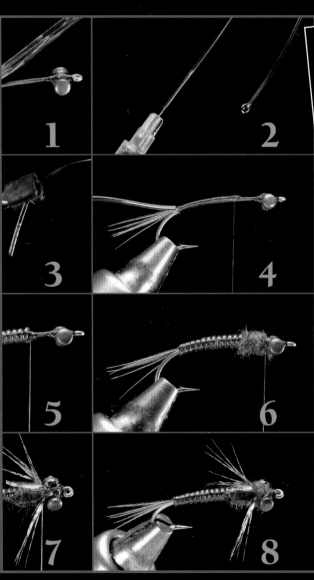